# How to survive a long haul flight

# Hello

No matter where I'm flying long haul I always end up pondering how a huge combination of metals and plastics, carrying over three hundred people is able to hurtle through the air at over 500 miles an hour at thirty thousand feet. It's not right really, is it? How does this giant bird soar through the air without flapping its wings? How does it takeoff and land so smoothly? Every single flight I wonder the same questions and always conclude that I don't know, I don't want to know, I don't need to know and, as long as I get to my destination, I don't really care.

Then I try and go to sleep, I never do.

# How to survive a long haul flight

*Matthew Eaves*

**How to Survive a Long Haul Flight**

*Second Edition, November 2008*

First published in the United Kingdom by Mandival:

http://www.mandival.co.uk

Written by Matthew Eaves:

http://www.mattheweaves.co.uk

Book web site:

http://www.longhaulflighttips.net

Cover and layout by Alexander Blanc:

http://www.allrollover.co.uk

Cover photograph used under 'Creative Commons' licence; image adapted from original by flickr.com user René Ehrhardt:

http://www.flickr.com/photos/rene_ehrhardt

http://www.flickr.com/photos/rene_ehrhardt/2391114010

ISBN: 978-0-955-9844-0-2

*For Justina... the reason to fly back.*

# Acknowledgements

Many people have been involved in this book and I want to thank them for their help, support, patience, advice and involvement during the three years it took to research and write.

Thanks to editors Nikki Fox, Hal MacLean, Doreen Sorrell and Derek Sorrell who have put in countless hours suggesting revisions, correcting typos and keeping me on task when I wander.

Alexander Blanc, thank you for designing the layout and original cover, and thank you to René Ehrhardt for agreement to use one of your photographs on the cover of this second edition.

Andrew Eaves, my brother, thank you for being a part of the final proof reading team, and putting together the index.

Hais Deakin, thank you for continued support with the web site.

Special thanks to key contributors (in no particular order): Richard Pont, Katy Wills, Lucy from the cabin crew, Geraint Lang, Sarah Davey, James Taylor, Graham Hart, Jonathan Furness, and all the other people from around the world who read and contributed to the original internet blog post and forum with tips, advice, thoughts and suggestions.

I should also thank Justina and my parents who have been very patient with me while I've been typing away in small dark rooms, and not come out for hours.

# Flight Plan

# Introduction

## Flying start

December has finally arrived and Justina and I are finally resting in a holiday lodge in Norfolk. After a busy few months we decided to take some time away between Christmas and the New Year to stop and relax. We're staying in a cottage that has views over a lake currently scattered with ducks and swans. The sun has just set and the water was ablaze in a deep orange. In a few hours we'll drive the short journey to the city of Norwich and explore rows of quaint shops before finding a restaurant and having something to eat.

The place we are staying is just two hours by road from our hometown and I often wonder why we board big planes and fly half way round the world when enjoyable and relaxing places exist so close to our roots.

Just recently we boarded a long haul flight to Florida and enjoyed excellent in-flight customer service from an airline that appeared to be genuinely passenger focused. We had never travelled with the airline before and they made everything about our journey so easy, comfortable, relaxing and bearable. I loved the experience so much that if they offered a service on a future route that I planned to travel on, I'd fly with them by preference.

On the way home I detested the airline. Same plane, same seat, same service, but I disliked the huge queue standing between us and the understaffed check-in desks at the airport, right through to the chaos involved in boarding the aircraft. My seat felt uncomfortable, the quality of the in-flight meal was poor and the time taken for the in-flight crew to collect meal trays was unacceptable. Arguably, in the airlines defence, I was disappointed to be going home after such a great holiday, tired, irritated and sun burnt.

I guess what I am trying to say here is that no two flights are ever the same and for moments throughout your flying careers you'll experience amazing customer service while feeling at a terrible level of discomfort.

You really need to read this book from cover to cover if you want to get a picture of what to expect, but nothing can beat the actual first hand experiences you'll discover for yourself. You'll either really detest it...

> *"I hate flying, I always end up squashed, smelly, irritated, tired, exhausted, and broke."*

> **Hayden**

Or love it...

> *"I actually enjoy the flights..... the thrill of adventure, the prospect of seeing my loved ones again, having food (of sorts) delivered to my seat and not having to clean up after, time to myself to think, to re-evaluate my direction in life, to read, to look out the window at weird and wonderful countries, to enjoy the privilege of my place in this world that means I get to travel like this... all the other stuff is part of the challenge."*

> **Gina Revill, New Zealand**

## Cabin fever

My first long flight was back in 1997, from London's Heathrow to O'Hare International in Chicago. The journey was only eight and a half hours long and I remember feeling squashed, smelly, irritated, tired, exhausted and incredibly bored. Since then I've flown long haul all over the globe for my job.

One of the few downsides of my work is the limited funding when it comes to air travel. I was sent on a business trip to New Zealand by 'economy class' and I estimated the b2b (bed to bed) time would be about 36 hours. I had absolutely no idea how or what I should prepare to make what became nearly a forty-hour journey more bearable.

Having survived the uncomfortable initial flight, I was then challenged by a shower-less transit stopover, and felt very sticky and started to smell. On the second flight sleep deprivation became a bigger irritation and all I could do was think of ways to make the journey home less straining. I learnt lots about the 'not so easy' way to fly and have since tried out my tips, along with tips shared by others on lots of flights worldwide.

Prior to learning the hard way, the first thing I did to prepare for the New Zealand trip was to go down to my local library to find a book giving advice on long haul journeys, I couldn't find one. The nice lady in the local bookshop also did a search, nothing.

Next I headed over to the internet and had a look around for advice and tips for long haul flying. A few people had written short blog entries here and there, but nothing substantial offering advice to make the journey more pleasant. I'm still astounded that we've been travelling by plane for decades, yet I couldn't find advice for a long airborne journey.

Being a researcher at the time, I then decided to conduct my own research project asking many experienced travellers for advice on flying long haul. Once I'd got some sound advice I'd then start a blog entry listing the tips. Next stage was to try out the tips when flying myself and add any new ones I discovered whilst on my journey.

I researched, reviewed and shared what I found out via the internet and launched a blog entry entitled 'Tips to Survive a Long Haul Flight'. The resulting impact was astounding and within a few weeks of writing I had hundreds of visits each day. By the time this book was going to press over half a million people had read the entry, lots contributing their own tips, ideas and experiences.

At one point I had to move the page onto a faster server to cope with demand. It has since moved again, twice. You'll be able to see it in its current form at: http://www.longhaulflighttips.net where you'll also be able to add your very own tips, advice and journey experiences to what has now turned into quite a big resource. I'll consider any submissions you make for inclusion in the next revision of this book, if there is a second edition that is. Hey, tell your friends and family to buy a copy! Purchase another one and send it to your Auntie Sheila in Australia, she can have a read and come and visit you!

Not all the information in this book is available on the web site, you'll find out substantially more here, including information from a check-in assistant and a member of a flight crew. You will find some interesting links to web sites, and will probably be spending hours searching around the internet to read associated information.

All web sites included in this book were live at time of publication. In the event of a referenced web site going offline check out the excellent http://archive.internet.org and simply enter the failing internet address into the search bar, hopefully the archive will be able to take you back in time.

Scattered throughout the book are tips, some are mine, some are friends and some are by the visitors of the original blog entry.

Here is a tip by someone called Marg...

> *"I have found my chances of actually getting some sleep are increased if I have a window seat. This way I have something to lean against without worrying that I am going to collapse onto some unsuspecting poor soul's shoulder. I also like to be almost the last person onto the flight. The reason for this is to check out where everyone is seated. If I happen to see some vacant areas I check with the crew and after takeoff move to a roomier spot."*
>
> ***Marg***

I'll do my best to keep this forerunner to your adventure as light hearted as possible, and drop in some stories, both mine and from friends, colleagues and family.

Flying is a trying and tiring experience but can also be a lot of fun, you'll meet some great people, share some wonderful experiences and bring home amazing memories. Above all, there is nothing like the feeling you get when you've had a great trip and then climb back into your own bed when you get home.

So, first things first, where in the world are you right now?

## I'm waiting for takeoff...

OK, if you're about to takeoff one of my colleagues swears by yawning as a way of getting your hearing back after your ears do that popping thing.

## I'm in the air...

You'll probably want to jump now to chapter five and take on board some of the tips, once you've read them come back to the start and see if you've forgotten anything! You might also learn some stuff that will help you with future trips.

## I'm going to board the plane soon...

Board quickly if you want your hand luggage stored in the compartment with limited space above your seat (easy access during the flight), board slowly if you are not so fussed where it is stored.

If you're wearing a jacket or coat, ask the steward or stewardess to hang it on a hanger for you, and be quick in asking for a pillow, they will be in limited supply.

Have your boarding pass ready and your passport open at the page with that dodgy looking photograph of you that you'd rather people did not see. Listen carefully for your row number, it will be announced when its time for you to board.

## I'm planning to fly long haul, I've bought my ticket...

Jump to chapter two. When you've finished the book you might want to read chapter one for some ideas on ticket booking in the future.

## I'm planning to fly long haul, not bought a ticket or packed...

OK, start from here! Flying is not daunting, its good fun, even enjoyable if you take the time to read this book! I'll try and help you pick a ticket, give some packing advice, list off items you should definitely pack and then advise you on some tips for surviving the long haul. I'll try and explain everything as simply as possible and make the whole process fun.

## I missed the plane!...

Don't panic. Be very nice to the airport staff, it's probably not their fault that you missed the plane. We miss planes for all sorts of reasons, the biggest problem being traffic accidents on the roads feeding the airports. Just don't get angry! I find the nicer you are the more willing the airlines are to help you. We all have our bad days.

# 1

# Booking

**"To know the road ahead, ask those coming back."**
*Ancient Chinese Proverb*

## Budget

Before we go any further it is essential to get the money formalities over with.

When travelling I often dread to check my bank account to see just how much the unexpected costs are eating into the balance. Great trips don't end when you get back, they end when you've paid for them, so don't let that be months or even years after you return. Work out a budget and stick to it.

> *"Sit down with a pen and figure out exactly how much you want to invest in your trip and how much money you have to do so, I'm still paying off a holiday I took three years ago by seriously overspending while away."*

> **Jane**

If you plan on borrowing funds work out just how long it will take you to pay it back, along with how much interest you are paying for this privilege.

On a typical trip you might consider some of the following points to impact on finance:

- flight tickets;

- insurance;

- holiday products (including clothing);

- travel to and from the airport;

- airport parking;

- airport food;

- tax free shopping;

- transfers;

- car hire;

- accommodation;

- gift purchases (including impulse buys);

- meals;

- excursions.

Whatever you expect to spend, it will almost certainly be more. Keep absolutely on top of your finances at all times and you'll enjoy your time away without the fear of having to pay it off later.

Lets not forget that you are away from home you will save some money too which is usually consumed by your everyday life. Factor into your budget the money you've saved, such as petrol costs, the commute to work, and the weekly food bill.

## Obey the system

I remember one steward speaking through the PA system whilst on a budget airline flight somewhere over Europe. He announced something along these lines while airborne over Europe:

> *"Good afternoon ladies and gentlemen, there is a passenger currently smoking in the rear section toilets. Passengers are reminded that this airline operates a strict no smoking policy and the offending passenger will be asked to leave this plane immediately. Passengers are also reminded that when this plane lands the 'seat belt' sign will remain on until the captain switches it off.*

*I will accept any customers undoing their seat belts and standing up prior to the switching off of the 'seat belt sign' as enthusiastic volunteers wishing to help me clean the plane. Thank you; enjoy the rest of your flight."*

**Flight Steward**

If only every member of an aircrew could be as light hearted as this chap when it came to getting over important messages with a touch of humour.

Needless to say, everybody was looking over his or her shoulders scornfully watching the offending smoker shuffle quietly back to her seat. Eyes then shot between the steward and the smoker as they exchanged glares. I love airline staff, I think they work hard while constantly surrounded by us sometimes miserable and difficult passengers all demanding personal attention, and yet another drink.

*"I watched a passenger being removed from the aircraft prior to take off because he was intoxicated and being offensive to the aircrew trying to manage the situation. It was really annoying because his stupidity meant the plane was delayed while his baggage was located and removed."*

**Jackson**

From the very first moment you start your booking, to the moment you get home, you should always take travelling as seriously as possible. Never be late, always obey the rules of the airport and airline, and be courteous to fellow passengers and staff, it really helps. If you do these things, you'll have a better trip, guaranteed.

## Fit to travel

Before you now invest some of your budget, are you physically able to make flights? You'll need to let any airline you book with know well in advance of any specific needs that you have, as you might need clearance to fly, especially if assistance is needed for you on board including use of medical equipment during the flight.

Most airlines will not require medical clearance for those who have a condition considered permanent or stable. Medical clearance will probably be required if you have been subject to a recent illness, injury, surgery, hospitalised, are travelling to reach treatment, or have an existing medical condition which is unstable. Always seek advice from your doctor if you are in doubt.

British Airways have a dedicated 'Passenger Medical Clearance Unit', which gives support and advice for their passengers requiring information on this subject. More information can be found via the information tab on the British Airways web site at http://www.ba.com. Other good airlines should be able to advise too.

The http://www.everybody.co.uk/airindex.htm web site is a resource that provides airline-by-airline information on the services each carrier offers, including specific needs for medical clearance. The site provides information for most major airlines and lots of smaller carriers, including short haul flights. Visiting the site and clicking at random on one of the airlines listed we learn about their services.

The randomly selected airline:

- can provide for special dietary requirements if notified 72 hours before departure (an additional charge may apply);

- cannot carry guide dogs;

- is unable to carry stretchers;

- states manual wheelchairs and electric wheelchairs with dry cell batteries can be carried in aircraft hold (free of charge and must be arranged at time of booking);

- provide meet and assist staff;

- requests any assistance required should be agreed with the pre-flight department at time of booking.

If you are **pregnant** it is advisable to speak with your doctor before flying, check out the following internet site for good advice or pregnant travellers:

> *"Some airlines won't allow you to travel for 30 days before your due date, while others won't let you on board if your due date is less than seven days away."*

> ***http://www.pregnancy-info.net***

The site also points at recommendations by the American College of Obstetricians and Gynecologists who in turn recommend that women don't fly after their 30th week of pregnancy, the web site at: http://www.acog.org has further information.

Diabetes UK offer advice and guidance for **diabetics** about to fly, search for 'air passengers' in the search box on their web site (http://www.diabetes.org.uk), it is really useful. At the end of the article is a telephone number for further support. Diabetes UK have also been proactive in offering advice to airline catering companies.

The Guide Dogs for the Blind Association is a well-established charity that works tirelessly to help and improve the lives of people who are **blind** or **partially sighted**. They are mainly known for their funding and training of guide dogs, but also work to raising awareness, seek rights, opportunities, and responsibilities for those they work for and they also fund research. Visit the http://www.guidedogs.org.uk web site and enter 'advice when travelling abroad' into the search box for an article which includes:

- obtaining a 'Pets Passport';

- arranging travel;

- travelling by ferry, hovercraft or 'Eurotunnel Shuttle Services';

- travelling by air;

- travel preparation;

- advice while abroad.

There is lots of further useful information on the web site, enter 'international flights' into the search box for more advice.

If you are **deaf** or suffer from a **hearing impairment** check with the airlines for information they offer and services provided. The http://www.deaftravel.co.uk web site is a good place to find information and advice.

Speak with a doctor before you book if you are concerned about medical related issues.

## Research

You've probably already got a good idea about where you want to visit, researching that destination and how you are going to get there is an essential part of any trip. The following sites will help you refine your ideas and make decisions...

- http://www.airlinequality.com - reviews airports, airlines, seats, lounges and more.
- http://www.who.int - information from the World Health Organisation, a good place to find out more about the attributes which can cause ill health when travelling (the following report is interesting: http://www.who.int/ith/en).
- http://www.tripprep.com - trip preparation advice.
- http://www.nature-blog.com - well worth a read, all about nature, travel and vacation.
- http://www.bugbog.com - help with holiday planning including maps and tours.
- http://www.holidaycare.org.uk - UK based travel and information service for the disabled and older people.
- http://www.backpacker.com - excellent site for those planning to back pack.
- http://www.thetravelinsider.info - web site to help save money, make better travel choices and travel more comfortably.
- http://www.tripadvisor.com - more than 10 million reviews of hotels, holidays and locations by travellers.
- http://www.travellersconnected.com - a place to talk with people who live at the destination, who has been there, who is currently there, and who is thinking of travelling there too.
- http://www.wayn.com - find others who will be going to the same place that you are, and share with friends back home what you are doing.
- http://www.holidaywatchdog.com - holiday reviews from those that have already been.
- http://www.travel-library.com - user reviews and travelogues.

- http://www.sharetrip.com - reviews, videos and photographs.
- http://www.wikitravel.org - a wiki site made for travellers by travellers.
- http://www.world66.com - a good travel experiences site.
- http://www.travellerspoint.com - guides, blogs, reviews and help.
- http://www.bugbitten.com - plan, search and read reviews.

# Class

There are four main types of ticket to fly by:

- 'First Class' is the highest quality and most exclusive seating available. A-list celebrities, multi-millionnaires, CEO's and senior government ministers will rub shoulders with each other while drinking champagne;
- 'Business Class', high quality, aimed at business travellers and usually the highest level on international flights on many airlines;
- 'Premium Economy', slightly better Economy Class with usually more legroom between seats; and
- 'Economy Class' (also known as 'Standard' or 'Coach') is basic accommodation and commonly the preferred and most cost-effective seat for leisure travellers.

> *"I'm just off round the world on a bucket class ticket, much as I hate it, I just couldn't justify doubling the price for the sake of a few more inches and the same crap food."*
>
> ***David***

So what are business and first class ticket holders getting other than more roomy seats compared to those of us who travel economy? They get access to free travel lounges at the airport, including showers, food, drinks and comfy chairs. Few long haul travellers realise that at the half way transit airport there are independently run travel lounges, which they can pay a small fee to 'join' for the transit period and include food, drinks, comfy chairs and a shower!

## Who should I book with?

Money is hard to earn, and we're all looking for ways of getting ourselves from A to B and back again for as little cost as possible. I much prefer to spend money at the destination, than on the cost of getting there, I am a bargain hunter.

> *"Ask friends and neighbours in your town which agent they book through and the kind of service they encounter."*
>
> **Greg**

So how do we:

- pick an airline which is value for money;

- know what is a great price for the planned travel route; and

- find out what kind of service we will receive?

Picking a booking agent is usually quite simple. Start off by exploring the travel shops in your town remembering that they will constantly be asking you for your contact details so they can follow up your initial enquiries. If you visit five travel agents to compare prices, expect five travel agents telephoning you to chase your business. The way I get around this issue is to simply not give my telephone number to anyone.

> *"Some airlines offer 'AVOD' services, which stands for 'Audio Video on Demand'. I prefer to fly with these carriers as the airlines that don't offer 'AVOD' usually start the film soon after take off, and that is when I prefer to sleep. I like to watch a film towards the end of the flight, pausing it when I pop to the toilet or need to stretch my legs."*
>
> **S. Geoffreys**

On the internet you'll find loads of great deals from companies selling packages and flights, but they might not be selling seats on all the airlines that fly to your destination, so shop around. Compare the agents, compare the web companies.

> *"If you are very big like me make sure you tell the booking agent as some airlines insist I book two seats, often the second seat is discounted."*
>
> **Big Dave**

When travelling long haul you'll usually fly into another season. You may fly from summer to winter and find lots of attractions and tourist driven services are closed up, hence the reason the ticket was so cheap.

> *"Some tickets are less expensive when take off is at an unsociable hour, it is worth consider these flights as travel to the airport is often easier with less traffic on the roads."*
>
> **Sean**

Some prices will include airport taxes, some won't, some will include in-flight meals, and some won't. You'll need to ask for the final figure for each seat, you might even have to pay extra to be certain you'll be seated with your friends and family. Remember if a flight deal seems too good to be true, it often is.

Talking of flights, there are two main kinds you can book...

## Charter flights

Charter flights are often bundled in as part of a package holiday. If you book a package holiday you'll usually get flights, transfers and hotels all included in the one price.

Charter flights operate out of regular airports and usually at scheduled times, but they will only fly if enough seats have been sold on the plane. Usually the holiday company running the package holiday deal will block buy all or most of the seats, and if enough seats are sold the plane will fly. If too few seats are sold the trip could be cancelled, this means that you will be offered a refund or another date.

> *"Charter flight dates are usually not very flexible, meaning you won't have as much choice on your return date, as you would with a scheduled flight."*
>
> **Nick**

I've heard lots of bad things from people about charter airlines offering a lower quality of service, less legroom and sometimes planes that are well worn and could do with a refit. Personally, I've found charter flights to be good experiences, friendly staff, nice food, even if I do have to pay extra on some airlines for drinks. I've never had a flight cancelled and have bought tickets at very low prices. One negative is that charter flights can be cancelled as little as ten days before flying, a second negative is that I've only ever been on a full charter plane; there is rarely an empty seat.

> *"Share prices your have been quoted from companies with their competitors, see if a price can be beaten. They often match or beat. I go with the company that offers the best service for the lowest price."*
>
> ### Jenny, Swanage

Some of the charter companies fly to airports which are not accessed by scheduled airlines, and therefore charter airlines can be proudly credited for opening up new routes to passengers.

Some haulage airlines, usually carrying cargo sometimes offer a limited number of passenger seats on flights to their destinations;

- http://www.aircharterguide.com is a pretty informative site with search features available for charter flights;

- http://www.charterflights.co.uk might be of interest to UK based passengers; and

- http://www.globalplanesearch.com is a site with aircraft for sale and available for private charter if you're feeling really rich.

> *"Charter is all about backsides on seats, so some charter airlines will sell those seats without the encouraged package holiday deal if that means that they are going to get more people on the flight, so it is worth asking for 'flight only' when talking with a travel agent."*
>
> ### Steve

In recent years, there have been cases where charter airlines have gone bust and left some passengers stranded at their destinations, it is always advisable to take out insurance that covers the cost of getting home. If you can be flexible the charter flight might be the way forward for you.

Before booking with a charter airline, ask yourself the following questions...

- What implications (work holiday date changes, hotel cancellations, connecting journeys) will there be if the charter airline decided to cancel the ticket?

- If the flight is cancelled can I afford to pay a potentially higher fee for alternative seats on a scheduled airline?

- What happens if I cancel? Charter airlines policies for cancellations are usually quite strict and you won't always get all your money back?

So, if you've booked the time off work, sorted out your lift to the airport, organised someone to feed Barry the cat, arranged accommodation at your planned destination, and then you get a letter to say your flight has been cancelled, would it matter? If yes, then you'll probably need to book a scheduled flight in the first place.

> *"I found a significant financial saving by booking two single tickets with different airlines. I flew to New York from London Heathrow Airport via British Airways, and flew home with United to London Gatwick."*

> *Yu*

## Scheduled flights

Scheduled flights are bought either through the airline directly, or through a travel or booking agent. When enquiring you'll be given a quote on how much a seat is going to cost and then you'll be able to book straight away.

> *"The price will usually increase as the date of the flight gets nearer, unless the airline is having difficulty filling the plane and lowers its seat prices."*

> *Ben*

Unlike charter flights the scheduled ones often have many slots to the same destination, at the same times, every day. Be sure to check the prices of all the slots and airlines for the day you wish to fly.

*"You'll find that an airline ticket can be a lot cheaper at certain times of the year, including when children are not on school holiday and towards the end of a tourist season."*

**Dick**

Different airlines have what I like to call 'hidden costs' in their price structures, you might find that an airline will quote you a price to fly, but then, as mentioned before, charge you more money to sit together or have an in-flight meal. Some airlines are still to add airport tax charges to the cost of the flight too.

*"For all flights you should enquire at the booking stage if you plan to sit with your partner, family or friends."*

**Joanna T**

When booking a flight ask about the airline's cancellation policy, you might lose all or some of the money you pay if you cancel. If the airline will not refund you in full then consider taking out a travel insurance policy, this will cover sudden cancellations.

*"Scheduled airlines often have the latest films on board and frequent visits of the drinks cart, which is usually free."*

**Keith B**

If you are flying to a far away destination, which will involve a transit stop en route, chances are you won't find a charter flight solution and will have to book a scheduled flight.

Have a good look around the various travel agents and internet sites for flight prices:

- http://www.travelocity.com
- http://www.lastminute.com
- http://www.expedia.com
- http://www.flightcentre.co.uk
- http://www.skydeals.co.uk
- http://www.cheapflights.co.uk

- http://www.airline-network.co.uk
- http://www.statravel.co.uk - great for travelling young people
- http://www.opodo.co.uk
- http://airninja.com - for discount airlines worldwide
- http://www.thinkflights.com
- http://www.farecast.com
- http://www.trailfinders.com - ideal for the independent traveller
- http://www.cheapseats.com
- http://www.cheaptickets.com
- http://www.travelling.com

Some of the above listed web sites are consolidators. A consolidator is an intermediary company that buys tickets (usually in bulk) at discount from the airline; we benefit from their significantly discounted rates. Consolidators have gained respect amongst air travellers in recent times but some have been known to go bust overnight causing chaos for their customers. If you are buying from a consolidator ensure you understand the cancellation charges as they can be less flexible in comparison to those bought from travel agents, or direct from the airline. Consolidators also bulk purchase tickets from charter airlines.

> *"Find significant savings by flying at an unpopular hour of the day, also check various airline promotions and incentives."*
>
> *Mo*

If you are looking for a really cheap flight, how about becoming an air courier?

# Air couriers

Parcel and package couriers all over the world use humans to speed up package deliveries. Check out http://www.aircourier.co.uk as a way of reaching a destination at a discount, transporting a package.

The web site states the following:

> *"What we do for members: Using the latest technology the IAATC keeps track of every courier company in the world that requires couriers and regularly distributes this information to members. Information on last-minute flights in the UK is sent by e-mail to members, this is also posted daily on our computer in the USA. Members can access the computer by fax or computer 24 hours a day.*
>
> *The air courier: Couriers need to be fit, reliable, independent individuals over 18 years of age of any nationality.*
>
> *How does it work?: Many tons of cargo travel with couriers every week, unlike regular cargo it clears customs on arrival. This results in the cargo arriving at its destination sooner which is essential for time sensitive material."*

> ***http://www.aircourier.co.uk***

And for those seeking a longer adventure with cargo, how about a cruise? Http://www.cargoshipvoyages.co.uk have some available.

## Which airline?

This is a very good question. I like to travel with an airline company based to the country of the final destination, I believe it makes the break away from home that little bit longer when I fly with the culture I am visiting. So, if I'm off to Thailand I fly by Thai Airways, and if I'm off to New Zealand, it's Air New Zealand, Quantas for Australia, and so on. Being a bargain hunter I still always consider the airline offering the lowest price.

> *"As I handed over my money I imagined a sweet smelling cabin, sparsely furnished with reclining chairs with built in television playing the latest blockbusters whilst being served the finest food and drinks, laughing and having a great time on my way. The only element of this dream that was actually realised was that I would arrive at my destination, eventually.*
>
> *I can remember stepping onto the plane, gliding through*

*first class, eagerly looking for my seat, eventually stepping into economy. I could only compare my disappointment to wandering though Narnia, all happy and excited at the fairy tale where lions talk and half-man half-goats roam freely before stepping back into a grotty old wardrobe. I didn't realise you could get so many people on an aeroplane, it was rammed. The seats where no more than garden recliners and there was only one television for the whole cabin!*

*I strapped myself into my chair and awaited the safety video which looked like it had been filmed in a poorly decorated restaurant sometime during 1973. 'Upon hearing the instruction, please extinguish your cigarette in your armrest ash tray and calmly place your life vest over your head before pulling the orange toggle for inflation.' If was then quite clear that I was flying with the last airline in the world to allow smoking on board. The whole journey was rather more like a coach trip than an international flight, and my seat would not recline.*

*I do a lot of research into airlines these days, before I make the booking!"*

**James Taylor, Norwich**

Different airlines offer different deals and services. I find a great place to go and get an idea of what an airline is actually like by visiting http://www.airlinemeals.net. On the site you will find hundreds of pictures of meals taken by passengers just before they are about to consume them, the pictures are then shared on the site for future flyers to see what has been served before.

*"I needed to get from London to Chicago as cheap as possible, it meant a longer journey, and flying via Paris, but saved me over £100."*

**Lorne**

Lots of travellers have left airline reviews over at http://www.airline-reviews.co.uk which makes interesting reading. Go there and add your own airline reviews after your flights are over. If you are vegetarian, vegan or have any specific dietary requirements you'll need to tell the person you book with and organise your special meal.

Http://www.flightcomparison.co.uk and http://www.skyscanner.net are web sites I've used in the past to search for the best price for specific routes.

> *"When you book your flight, if you ask for a special meal you will get served first, then you can finish before everyone and beat the post-meal rush to the loo."*
>
> *Anon*

## Feedback, complaining and congratulating

Writing your experiences and opinion for others to read really helps, and I won't travel anywhere until I've read the reviews and opinions of those that have been before me. The internet has become a tool which has given a voice to the man on the street, and with the power of people writing their own blog and posting in forums there has evolved a whole new medium of reviewers, writing about everything and anything they experience in their lives. So share what you learned about your trip with others.

Lots of web sites exist which are dedicated to collecting together reviews, opinions and experiences. Find one you like and add to it, remember to justify honestly any opinions you have as these sites are public places, don't get personal.

> *"Tot up the actual total cost of a low cost alternative airline before you book. Ask about the extras, meal costs, fuel supplements, seat reservations. I fly budget whenever I can."*
>
> *Richard the Trekker*

Not everyone will experience the perfect trip and may need to make a complaint. Complaining effectively is a skill, and needs to be managed carefully...

- Put your complaint in writing and avoid telephone complaining where possible. If you do need to talk on the telephone document the name and extensions of the people you talk to.

- Complain to a real person, find out the name of the relevant person charged with dealing with complaints and write to them. Mark the envelope as private and confidential.

- Research your consumer rights in advance of your complaint, reference them in your letter.

- Write a clear and factual record of events in correspondence, try to keep to the point.

- State in your first letter what you are seeking to achieve by complaining.

- Include copies (never originals) of documents and photographs that support your complaint.

- Be persistent, if you don't get the response you are happy with request the name of someone higher in the organisation, such as the Managing Director or CEO.

- Stay calm when writing, even if you are cross.

The UK Consumer Direct web site offer advice and letter templates to help the British complain: http://www.consumerdirect.gov.uk.

The BBC have also put together a very good resource about how to complain: http://www.bbc.co.uk/consumer/how_to_complain.

As consumers we are often quick to complain, but often fail to say 'well done'. When you've had a great experience tell people about it, write to companies to tell them what they did good, and write great reviews on the travel review web sites for others to read.

# Budget revolution

'No Frills' has become a whole new option for the modern day traveller. In the UK and Australia there has been a lot of competition between newly emerging budget airlines on short hop distances at very low costs to the passenger. The larger airlines are now having to consider their positions as increasing numbers of budget airlines take to the sky and are starting to challenge the long haul routes, offering the same distances at a lower cost.

No frills airlines cut the levels of service they provide in order to fly at a lower operating cost, often claiming to return the saving on to you, their valued customers. On a no frills flight, if you want one, you might have to pay for your meals and drinks separately, consider taking your own food on board with you.

> *"If you are from the UK check that your holiday is ATOL protected, visit http://www.cca.co.uk, our holiday company went bust one year, but we got our money back."*
>
> **Trev**

Leg space will also be an issue when it comes to budget airlines. You might be challenged with even less leg space than you anticipated as the budget airline will attempt to fit more seats within the cabin of the plane.

Check if the airline stops on route to your destination. The flight might first travel in the direction of another destination to pick up more passengers before heading to the final destination. Factor in the time added to your journey.

> *"Explore the internet, find out what other people think about the airline you plan to travel with. I like to think that the airlines themselves also search around for comments about their service and take notice of their passengers."*
>
> **J**

## Destination airport

Some budget airlines will fly to airports which are outside of main cities, rather than the main central city airport. They do this because either landing fees are cheaper for them or the major global airlines have the entire takeoff and landing slots tied up between them. Although the cost of your flight might be cheaper than flying into the main city airport you might find the cost of transfers (taxi, bus, train) will be more expensive, and also increase your travel time.

A good example is Florida in the United States. Florida includes the following airports landing international flights: Orlando International, Sandford, Fort Lauderdale, Fort Pierce St Luscie County, Jacksonville, Key West, Ocala and West Palm Beach. So when in the travel agents asking for a flight to Florida ask your agent to check all airlines that travel to all Florida airports, compare distances, and compare costs.

*"If you are going to Florida I find this page: http://tinyurl. com/6gptwo from http://www.undercovertourist.com really useful."*

**Jackie G**

Decide where it is you could stay once you have found affordable tickets, and the lowest price could be because the landing airport is a long distance from the tourist scene.

Consider:

- how much flights cost to the various airports;

- the distance to preferred accommodation from all potential airports;

- how much it will cost to travel from each airport to the accommodation; and

- the time it will take to travel from the airport to the accommodation.

*"I live in London and like to go to America three or four times a year to go on self drive road trips. I am unable to sleep on long flights and often find myself arriving very tired and groggy. I always spend my first night of sleep at the destination airport hotel before even attempting to get behind the wheel of a hire car."*

**Frank, London**

# Finding the best price

The simple rules to a great deal are as follows...

- Start your search as early as possible, but be conscious that as time passes prices of seats can increase and decrease depending on the popularity of the route. Many deals will involve making your reservation at least 21 days before the flight.

- Be flexible with dates and ask for the lowest fare.

- Last minute internet purchased flights can often create significant savings. These fares in some cases provide very little flexibility, read the terms carefully.

- Where prices are similar on the lowest two or three quotations check the details of each ticket, pick the ticket with the most flexible terms for cancellations and rescheduling.

- Flying very early morning before dawn can often create a significant saving.

- Use the same airline for the return journey, unless you can find two cheaper single tickets with two different airlines.

- Ask about senior and student discounts if you fall into either of these categories.

- Airlines need full planes, and may add discount seats to a flight without warning, keep checking prices.

> *"If when searching for flights online you find windows popping up on your computer screen congratulating you for being the 1,000,000th visitor to a particular web site and you've won an amazing free holiday, you haven't. It's just a trick to get you to phone a number and book. Don't fall for it."*
>
> **Gin**

## Fly the right way

When I book a long haul ticket, I ask three questions to the travel agent about journey length and jet lag, they are...

- What is the total journey time?

- Where does the plane stop on route (if at all) and how long for?

- Which way round the world does the aeroplane actually fly?

I believe when flying from the UK to New Zealand that it is better to fly the Asia route than the America route. Flying away from the setting sun is supposedly better than flying in the direction of daylight, I'm talking jet lag here and we'll address that little pest later.

> *"I use http://www.viewtrip.com to view my travel itinerary once the booking has been processed, I enter the reservation number and my surname and can view my information, it is great."*
>
> **Richard**

My brother and I got a great deal flying from London Heathrow to Chicago O'Hare in 2005. The trouble with the journey was that we had to detour through Atlanta airport, adding three hours to our journey each way. We saved about £200 each by taking that route, but ultimately a price was paid by the increased time spent in transit.

> *"Not exactly long haul, but if you need a connecting flight it might apply...*
>
> *One Irish budget airline have just started a web check-in, allowing you to do so up to 72 hours before you fly. The advantage to this is that you get a really good position in the boarding card numbers - most likely one of the very first to be called to board the plane (after passengers with special needs and children or priority boarding). Since these flights have notoriously low amounts of leg room in their seats, I make a bee line for the emergency doors and the seats there - loadsa room!"*
>
> **Halibut Fishface**

## Insurance

Insurance is critical when it comes to booking a journey and some airlines insist you have a valid policy. Most insurance companies organise their products in three levels labelled something like 'Gold', 'Silver', and 'Bronze'. Each of these services is a different price and the lower the price, the less benefits you get with the package. Always buy insurance which covers you for the duration of your journey.

> *"I already have European travel insurance cover included as a free perk by having a current account with my high street bank."*
>
> **Kevin, Sidcup**

Good point Kevin, and so do I, some credit card companies offer this service too. Also check if your current travel insurance cover expires while you are away travelling, voiding some of your trip from cover.

*"To win my business travel agents have often thrown in free travel insurance, it is usually the basic cover which I then pay to upgrade."*

**Dave**

It might be more cost effective to book the policy with an insurance broker than buy one of the travel agent's own insurance products. Read the policies carefully and examine the small print. Be sure to ask about your rights, cancellations (both at your choice and the airline's), and what happens if your luggage were to go missing?

*"Research other travellers' experiences. Http://www. dooyoo.co.uk is a very good UK consumer driven rating site for everything from electrical items to book reviews, http://www.ciao.co.uk is also worth a comparative visit."*

**Glenn**

## Fuel supplements

With the price of oil fluctuating across the world the impact on the airline industry has been increased fuel costs. Some airlines might add a supplementary charge for fuel, beyond the cost of your ticket. If applicable the charge will be collected by the airline prior to travel and covers the extra cost it has had to spend for increased fuel prices after your ticket was booked. I'm yet to hear of an airline who have returned money to passengers because the cost of fuel has dropped.

*"I usually find that the best deal for a ticket is one booked on the internet, although I always telephone the best quote company and speak to an agent or print out a quote and take it to travel agents and see if they can match it. I'm a little old fashioned and like to deal with a human when it comes to flight booking, I have lots of questions to ask."*

**Chelsea**

# Flight supplements

When booking a package holiday the price in the brochure might be subject to a flight supplement charge. These charges exist because airports are managed by different companies who charge airlines a premium each time they take off and land. With fees being different for each flight (depending on the location of the airport and time of day) holiday companies will often pass on this cost as a flight supplement.

> *"I've found that the brochure price for a holiday is often subject to extra charges which differ depending on which airport I fly from."*
>
> ***Kevin***

Ask if there is a flight supplement for airports within reasonable travelling distance from your home, factor in the cost of travelling to each airport against the flight supplement charge.

> *"Ask the booking agent to confirm exactly what time you should arrive at the airport before the flight, take copies of all the documents and receipts you are given for your trip, keep them in a safe place."*
>
> ***Jill***

# Tourist entry fee

When Justina and I head to Turkey we have to pay £10 each to enter the country on arrival. Apparently the fee is different depending on nationality. Not all countries charge an entry fee. Always have the right money ready, don't expect change.

> *"When I'm telephoning for quotes, and an agent takes ages to answer my call they automatically lose my business, I'd hate to have to ring them once I've booked to make an alteration or amendment and not be able to get through quickly and easily."*
>
> ***Terry***

## Tourist exit fee

500 Baht was the cost to leave Thailand in 2005, payable on exit at the airport, will you have to pay to leave? Ask your travel agent.

> *"Try not to book any flight until you are absolutely sure you can commit to the dates you want, await holiday confirmation from your employer. Also check that Auntie Merrill is able to visit and feed the cat as she could be on holiday at the same time you plan to be."*

**Vicki**

# 2

# Preparation

**"All things be ready if our minds be so."**
*William Shakespeare (Henry V)*

## Passport and visa

There are lots of things to do and think about before you ask Uncle Malcolm to drop you at the airport, lets start with passports. Some countries, like the United States, will not let you in if your passport is close to its expiry date. You'll need to check with your travel agent when you book how much time your passport needs to have remaining in order to fly to your final destination, it varies from country to country. It is good practice to replace a passport when it has six months left to expiry.

If going to the USA check out the following web site for the latest information on visa requirements visit the http://www. unitedstatesvisas.gov web site.

Generally three types of visa will be available:

1. Tourist Visa.

2. Working Holiday Visa.

3. Student Study Visa.

Use a search engine on the internet for the name of your country and the word 'visa'. Check out the official government advice, and be cautious of any dubious looking non-government web pages which offer to speed up a visa application.

Advice on passports and the application process can be found at:

- United Kingdom - http://www.ukpa.gov.uk
- USA - http://travel.state.gov
- Australia - https://www.passports.gov.au
- Canada - http://www.ppt.gc.ca
- Singapore - http://app.ica.gov.sg
- New Zealand - http://www.dia.govt.nz/diawebsite.nsf

For other countries use a search engine for the 'country name' and the word 'passport', your chosen search engine should then return a government link in the results. Follow your government's instructions and advice.

Some countries will require Visa applications in advance, especially if you plan to stay there for a long period or work there. Your booking agent will know the details for each country, also visit the web site of the government of the country you are visiting for more information.

Lots of passport applications are rejected because the applicant has forgotten to sign them, or has smiled in their photograph. Don't smile!

*"On Friday 6 August 2004, BBC News Online reported:*

*In the UK, you'll have to look morbid for an application to be successful. Toothy, open mouthed grins are being outlawed from the tiny 35mm by 45mm photographs because they will throw off scanners used at airports. Long fringes and head coverings, are also banned, under the new regulations along with dummies in babies' mouths. The new type of passports are being introduced in a bid to fight terrorism.*

*A Home Office spokesman said: "When the mouth is open it can make it difficult for facial recognition technology to work effectively." The machines work by matching key points on the holder's face, such as the mouth and eyes, with the photograph."*

***http://news.bbc.co.uk***

Of course this won't apply to all countries, but is a good guide on what to expect.

Photo machines are available at large railway stations and stores. These machines are set up with all the right lighting and backgrounds for passport pictures, and will usually let you take multiple pictures until you see one you like, and then print it for you.

When you're having a photograph taken for a passport your face should show a natural relaxed look, to do this:

- adjust the seat to the right height;

- don't wear a hat;

- take off glasses;

- keep your mouth closed;

- ensure you look straight at the camera with your eyes open;

- make sure the photo includes your full head from the top of your hair to just below your shoulders;

- the background for the photo should be a neutral colour, preferably white; and

- avoid shadows on your face and the background behind.

Once you receive your passport keep it in good condition, buy it a protective wallet. Tatty passports get lots of extra attention from foreign immigration officers, if they are falling apart immigration could consider the passport to be tampered with.

*"I watched a TV show which showed a family who had hand written their children's names onto their passports, something which is a complete 'no-no' in the United Kingdom. Writing on their passport resulted in them automatically becoming invalid for travel."*

**Jeff**

One of the longhauflighttips.net web site visitors, Julie, from Rochester in the UK, arranged for her son's passport to be replaced long before its actual expiry date as he had changed so much physically as he grew, visually he looked completely different to his passport picture. Decisions like this can help you through home and foreign customs much faster.

UK Post Offices offer British citizens a charged service where their staff check a completed application form is correct before it is sent off.

> *"If you are British and don't have enough time to sort a passport by post book and visit your nearest Passport Office, for a premium they will make it while you are there and you can leave with it a few hours later."*
>
> **Mike**

I've visited the office in London to have my passport replaced and it was a great experience. I telephoned the office in advance and was given a time slot to arrive, and a letter was sent to my home address confirming when I was expected. Upon arrival the man in front of me in the queue outside the building was turned away for being fifteen minutes early, they work absolutely to the clock.

Entering the building I was immediately searched and processed through airport style security. Next I was given a piece of paper with a unique number, a bit like the deli counters do in major supermarkets. The piece of paper told me to go to a waiting room on floor two, there were three floors of waiting rooms. I sat down, and deli counter style my number was called out telling me which window to go to.

I went to the window and my application was processed. I felt sorry for the man at the window to my left who was told his passport picture was not up to standard as he had cocked his head slightly in the image. He was sent off to join the other rejects in the queue for the photo machine at the end of the corridor.

I paid for my passport at another window and left. I'd paid for the seven day guaranteed postal service, I was so impressed that my new passport arrived the very next day at my home, even if the photo did make me look like a convict. More information on the British Passport Service is available from the http://www.ukpa.gov.uk internet address.

Whatever you do, obey your country's strict rules for owning a passport. Don't write on it (except where space is provided to write emergency contact details), look after it, and ensure you know where it is at all times. Oh, and make sure you take your new passport to the airport, not your old expired one, as some people do.

To summarise...

- Explore passport and visa requirements (ask your booking agent) that need preparing and approving before travel.

- Check the expiry date of your current passport if you have one, consider applying for another if you have six months or less remaining.

## Criminal convictions

Some countries will not allow you to enter if you have criminal convictions. It is critical that you are aware of any regulations and conditions that may affect your journey. Check with your booking agent if you are unsure of the restrictions you might face.

## Denied entry

If a country refuses you entry on your arrival, they will stamp your passport with their immigration stamp and then put a cross through the stamp to signify that you have been denied entry. They will then make arrangements to fly you home. The denied entry stamp will stay on your passport until it has expired and will probably raise questions at every destination you go to, and also when your passport is replaced.

## Currency

Arranging currency can be done with your travel agent, at the airport, at some post offices and you can also withdraw cash from many international ATM machines. Each method of withdrawing money will charge you some form of interest. Paying for goods and services with your credit or debit card is also an option you have available.

> "Exchange rates on currency goes up and down. I got a great deal buying US Dollars but the following week I bought more but did not get as much in exchange."
>
> **Maureen**

Check with your card issuing company to find out if your credit and/ or debit card will work at your destination. Also check if it will work at the transit airport which you might find yourself in half way to your final destination, you might smell and want to pay for a shower there. Check your credit card expiry date to make sure it does not expire before you return, contact the issuer to send out a new one to you if need be.

*"You'll need to take photographic ID when you buy travellers cheques. The 'Post Office' also offer travel money debit cards, I sometime use these on long trips."*

**Maureen**

Traveller's cheques are brilliant. You sign traveller's cheques twice, once in front of the person who sold them to you, and the second time when you swap them for local currency at your destination or to pay for goods or services. The trick with traveller's cheques is to keep your receipt separate from the actual cheques. If you lose either, you'll have the other to fall back on. Store the telephone number of the issuer to call if there is a problem .

*"Find out what the local currency is and how much things are going to cost (such as a typical evening meal) so you can plan spending budgets."*

**Ralph W**

Remember when buying foreign money you'll get a lower exchange rate for selling your unused foreign notes back into your own nation's currency, unless you strike a deal with the agent you buy from at the time of purchase.

*"I never buy local currency and I always use my credit and debit cards where possible, especially when paying for hotel costs. The negative side of not carrying cash is lots of fee charges for using my cards abroad."*

**Daniel**

I use a credit or debit card sometimes to pay for goods and services abroad, and also to draw cash from an ATM machine. One trick I've learned is to draw some money out of a cash machine and then use my mobile phone internet browser to log into my bank account and see what charge was incurred. This helps me decide if I am going to draw money out in a similar way in the future, although three lessons to learn here...

- Different banks charge different fees for drawing money from their ATM.

- Using a mobile phone to access the internet abroad is usually quite expensive.

- With so much spy-ware and hacking going on try and avoid logging into your bank account from an unfamiliar computer, such as an internet cafe.

An excellent free online currency converter is available online at: http://www.x-rates.com for you to check how much your money is worth abroad.

> *"Check your credit/debit card will work in the countries you are visiting."*
>
> **Joe**

# Card protection

Consider a card protection policy from your credit card issuer, in the event of your cards being lost or stolen an emergency number will be available for support. The policy will usually cover all of your cards, but if you have more than one credit card telephone all the issuers and find out what policies they offer, and how much they charge.

> *"Watch out for the hidden charges when using your credit card abroad, I bought a carpet in Australia and the interest rate for that transaction was higher compared to what the interest rate would have been in the UK."*
>
> **Spencer**

In the UK for around £15 per year you can have card care policies that include:

- a 24 hour emergency support number;

- all missing cards automatically ordered and dispatched;

- emergency cash advance to pay for personal belongings, accommodation and tickets home;

- support sourcing and replacing lost documents; and

- help to recover lost property or stolen keys.

The key recovery facility is great, you'll be given tags to put on your key sets. If the keys are found the finder simply puts them in a post box and the postal service will send them on to your card company for them to return. This is great in the UK, but I'm not sure what would happen if lost keys were dropped in post boxes in far away countries, ask when you take up the policy.

> *"Rather than carrying around a lot of cash I was withdrawing money from cash machines on my credit card, sometimes three times a day. I got the shock of my life when I returned to the UK to find I'd been charged £3 each time I'd used a cash point. The interest rate is also higher for the money I withdrew abroad. I cried."*
>
> *Barbara*

## Protecting belongings

Hundreds of thousands of bags go missing worldwide every month, an insurance policy will cover the loss of baggage.

To make things easier if baggage gets lost:

- ensure luggage can be clearly identified and has a tag stating where you live and where you are going;

- note down a description of the make, model, colour and distinctive markings for each item of luggage;

- place a copy of your itinerary and destination address on the inside, attached to the lid; and

- read in advance the advice of the UK Citizens Advice Bureau at http://tinyurl.com/5eebe4.

When unidentifiable baggage goes missing after a set period of time it gets auctioned off, disposed of, or destroyed.

Globalbagtag.com have offered a purchasable service since 1999, stating the following on their web site:

*"Our stylish heavy duty luggage tags and security stickers fix securely to your baggage. Full details of your luggage, travel itinerary and contact details are stored on our secure database and can be updated at any time."*

**http://www.globalbagtag.com**

Services like this are available from other companies too.

# Know the airport

The flight confirmation booking will tell you what time you have to arrive at the airport, but it is worth also researching the services and facilities available to keep you occupied while waiting for the flight:

- http://www.worldairportguides.com - for international airports;

- http://www.airportguides.co.uk - for UK airports;

- http://www.airport-maps.co.uk - for UK airport maps; and

- http://www.gofox.com/flights/airportmaps.php - for world airport maps.

# Sleeping in airports

I had to include a link to http://www.sleepinginairports.com which is 'the budget traveller guide to sleeping in airports', it is a very informative and entertaining site. Included in the site are traveller stories, experiences and information on places to sleep while waiting, very useful for delays and saving money on hotel rooms while waiting for a connecting flight.

# Airport parking

This is one of the most expensive charges you will need to pay, unless of course you are able to use public transport or grab a lift from Uncle Malcolm.

Parking is usually located some distance from the actual airport terminal, a bus service will usually be provided to transport to and fro. Once the car is parked expect to wait as long as fifteen minutes for the connecting terminal bus.

Some people are so late for their flights that I've seen them running from the long stay car parking areas towards the terminal with their luggage bouncing about behind them.

> *"I have missed a lot of flights by being late to the airport. I usually end up parking in the more expensive 'short stay' or 'medium stay' parking areas (rather than the more cost effective 'long stay') in order to save time, they are closer to the airport."*
>
> **Ben, Cambridge**

Some motoring breakdown service members will benefit from discounts on parking as a part of the membership privilege. How much money could you save by joining a breakdown service? For example, if it costs £45 to join for a year to save £40 on parking that is great value, and breakdown cover too!

> *"More than one parking company will often offer long stay parking at each airport, so compare prices. Online booking sometimes provides a discount too."*
>
> **Marvin**

## Non airport parking

Some airport parking deals are available from hotels near the airport that will include long stay parking with a nights booking. Shuttle bus services are usually available and provided by the hotel to transport customers between the hotel and airport. Hotel staff will drive your car to and from their hotel to a private secure parking area.

I once used this service and my car was returned covered in berries, leaves and was filthy. I reset the mileage counter when I left the car with the hotel, on return it had done 16 miles, I figure it had been parked eight miles away, in a bush.

> *"If we have an early flight we try and stay at a hotel near the airport the night before, this means travel to the airport is stress free for our family of eight."*
>
> **The Whites**

# Exercise

Exercise prior to air travel is good.

> *"Pre-flight Exercise*
>
> *The best form of exercise to achieve a high oxygen intake is one that makes use of the major muscle groups, such as jogging, running, squash, tennis, cycling and particularly swimming. To have any significant effect on oxygen saturation the exercise should be carried out three times a week for a period of 30 minutes. People in sedentary occupations should build up over a longer period, some six to eight weeks before a trip.*
>
> *The other type of exercise of interest to air travellers encourages circulation. Moderate dynamic exercise, such as brisk walking, not only decreases the tendency of the blood to clot but also exerts a protective influence on the circulatory system. Such an effect can last for several hours even after only 30 minutes exercise."*
>
> **http://www.aviation-health.com**

The Aviation-health web site is very comprehensive resource by a non-profit company promoting the health and well-being of airline passengers, take a look, they recommend eating muesli bars and sandwiches on arrival at your destination, presumably to combat jet lag.

If you are out of practice or unfamiliar with safe exercise you should always seek medical advice first.

# Legroom

Let's be honest, most travellers who are tall want the seat with lots of legroom, visiting the following web sites will help find them:

- http://www.seatexpert.com
- http://www.seatguru.com
- http://mobile.seatguru.com (view on a mobile).

Visual plans are available showing airline seating and in-flight amenities, complemented by airline information. Not all airlines are listed on the sites yet, but they do give detailed information on where great seats are on the different models of aeroplane, including colour coding to help identify superior and sub-standard seats, and comments on seats with limited recline, less legroom and misaligned windows. Seatguru.com also points out power points on some aircraft, essential for laptop users, like me.

> *"Usually you won't know the exact seat you will be sitting in on your plane until you 'check-in'. If your airline offers 'online check-in' up to 24 hours before the flight departs sometimes you can pick a seat online from home."*
>
> **Alice**

Http://www.uk-air.net/seatpitch.htm within the http://www.uk-air.net web site is also worth a look, it lists all the seat pitches for most airlines around the world.

> *"I'm really tall and I really don't like it when the person seated in front of me reclines their seat as soon as we're airborne. I do my best to get the front row seats in economy as otherwise I usually end up squashed up behind someone a lot shorter than me who feels the need to invade my space too."*
>
> **Dave**

> *"I think airlines should compromise the whole seat reclining debate by only allowing people to recline their seat if they are actually trying to sleep."*
>
> **Marie**

Various aircraft are made up of different seating layouts. For long flights the chances are you will be on a Boeing 747 aircraft which will usually be the following seat layout for economy class:

window - A, B, C - aisle - D, E, F, G - aisle - H, J, K - window

If we have been unsuccessful in finding seats with lots of legroom Justina and I ask for seats 'H' and 'J' over the wing, Justina likes to sit on the right hand side of the plane, and I find travelling over the wing more comfortable during turbulence. In these seats we also only disturb each other when either needs to go for a walk, but sadly lack a good view from the window.

> "When boarding the plane you'll have to place your hand luggage in the overhead storage. Some passengers are really annoying and insist on taking ages to do this by trying to retrieve something from inside their bag while standing in the aisle and blocking others trying to find their seat, when they could easily have located the thing they needed while waiting in the queue to board the plane."
>
> **Damian**

## Free upgrade

There are times when an airline has overbooked the number of economy seats and need to 'bump up' some passengers from economy to business class. The airline may also be bumping up business class passengers to first class. I don't think there is a single traveller who would not accept a free upgrade into business or first class if it were offered. Later we'll look at how to be picked for an upgrade, but for now, especially if you are travelling alone, you'll need to prepare for that moment.

Upgrade seats are generally in short supply. If you're a typical family travelling together, chances are you won't be upgraded, but sometimes children who are travelling alone are picked for those special seats so the airline staff can attend to their needs much more easily. The airline will reward the loyalty of its frequent flyers by priority, so if you're a member of the airline's 'frequent flyer programme' and happen to be travelling economy, the chances are, you'll be one of the first in line for an upgrade. You might be offered the upgrade in exchange for frequent flyer miles previously earned; a good offer but try and get the upgrade for free, chances are the airline has over booked its economy seats and needs to bump a few people up.

However, it's all about etiquette, if you look like you visibly won't fit in with the typically smart dress code of a business class cabin, then you won't be sipping tea from their china cups. If you are aiming for an upgrade the best thing you can do is to dress as smart, but as comfortably as possible. Obviously, if you are male don't fly in your best suit, unless you plan on wearing it again during your trip, as you'll need to transport it with you for the rest of the time away. Ladies, evening dress with your best hat would be seriously inappropriate.

Simply 'look smart', business class passengers are human too and usually appear slightly more casual when they travel. For the men, a tie-less shirt, smart trousers and smart clean shoes. For women, when picking smart clothing don't swap practical and comfortable shoes for heels. Smart hand luggage cases are also advisable, rather than rucksacks and plastic carrier bags.

If an air plane is overbooked, the airline will be looking out for travellers they can upgrade well in advance, so be early to the airport and be the first smart person they see. "Any chance of an upgrade?" is not a good line to use, try "Would there be any chance of a more roomy seat today?"

We'll revisit upgrading, and legroom in chapter four, Graham Hart thinks he knows how to do it.

## Preparing for travel sickness

I don't suffer from travel sickness, but my friend Geraint Lang from Wolverhampton does. Here is what he has to say on the subject:

> *"While travelling as a passenger in a car, plane or boat, have you suddenly felt quite hot, lost complete interest in your surroundings, and had no wish to further engage anyone in conversation, all because you had an overwhelming desire to be very sick?*
>
> *The last place you want to be in that situation is on a violently pitching deck of a boat, where the horizon keeps disappearing behind sickly green rolling waves that seem to continually strike against the side of the boat, further adding to the rocking motion of the craft, and exacerbating your feeling of sickness!*
>
> *Where do you go or what do you do in those situations, which for me can also occur on a train, or on board an aircraft, even on comparatively short flights? If you suffer in this way as a result of being a passenger, then you too are susceptible to travel or motion sickness.*

*Ever since I can recall, I have suffered from motion sickness. Fairground or amusement park rides that propel you rapidly in circles are a definite no-no for me-in such situations dizziness rapidly gives way to an overriding need to vomit. Things don't get any better even if I am sick, I then become totally overwhelmed by the desire to sleep. Often this lasts for a couple of hours, and when I wake I feel completely exhausted. Motion sickness is a totally debilitating experience for me.*

*The thought of the inevitable consequences of being a passenger in a vehicle usually mean that I tend to end up driving myself to most destinations. However, there are times when I have absolutely no choice in the matter, especially when I need to undertake a journey by coach, train or plane. In such situations, I take two precautionary measures, which seem to work!*

*I take a small, but highly effective anti-travel sickness tablet-the brand name is 'Kwells'. I have tried others, and only because I couldn't obtain Kwells - but these other brands had after effects, and caused me to fall asleep! Always check the label-better still ask a pharmacist whether there are any side-effects from taking such medication.*

*In conjunction with the Kwells, I wear 'Sea Bands' on both wrists. These are essentially wrist bands, but each one is fitted with a small solid plastic ball-bearing that when positioned correctly (roughly where a watch strap is worn), reproduces an acupuncture effect on the wearer by exerting a specific pressure on a part of the wrist immediately beneath the ball-bearing. Wearing Sea Bands seems to suppress the feeling of motion sickness!*

*Individually or using both methods together, I have found that I am spared the dire experience of motion sickness! Other members of my family have also benefited from the use of Sea Bands.*

*One further effective control of motion sickness-place a cool object behind the neck at the outset of a coach journey, especially on a hot day. It worked for me on a coach trip from Edinburgh to Inverness, when I'd forgotten to include the usual preventative items amongst my baggage-although in part the journey was made easier by the high quality of driving.*

*Perhaps Admiral Nelson might not have been so seasick at the outset of each voyage had he been able to access these remedies."*

**Geraint Lang, Wolverhampton**

*"If you suffer from travel sickness ask for a seat that is directly over the aircraft wing where I find less movement during turbulence."*

**Hubert, Ontario**

*"Take the travel sickness pill before boarding the flight rather than during the flight at the point where you start feeling sick."*

**June**

*"My grandmother was an avid cruise ship fanatic, she suffered from terrible motion sickness. When alive she swore by 'ginger root' to help prevent upset for her first few days at sea, I think of her each time I fly."*

**Marion**

The travel sickness pill is preventative, not reactive, always read the labels and seek medical advice if you are unsure.

## Jet lag preparation

Jet lag is horrible, and my advice is to get yourself prepared for the change in time zone two or three days before your journey. Http:// www.bodyclock.com is a good web site giving information on how to combat jet lag, it defines it as:

*"Jet lag is actually caused by disruption of your 'body clock', a small cluster of brain cells that controls the timing of biological functions (circadian rhythms), including when you eat and sleep. The body clock is designed for*

*a regular rhythm of daylight and darkness, so it's thrown out of sync when it experiences daylight and darkness at the 'wrong' times in a new time zone. The symptoms of jet lag often persist for days as the internal body clock slowly adjusts to the new time zone."*

***http://www.bodyclock.com***

The best aspect of the bodyclock web site is its 'Jet lag Calculator' which gives advice for your own specific journey. I'm planning a trip to Australia from London so I told the site that I'll be travelling through 10 time zones and usually wake up at 8am each day, bodyclock gave me the following advice:

*"TRAVELLING WEST: SEEK BRIGHT LIGHT between 16:30 (4:30pm) and 19:30 (7:30pm) then SWITCH to AVOID LIGHT until 23:30 (11:30pm). On DAY 2 SEEK BRIGHT LIGHT between 19:30 (7:30pm) and 22:30 (10:30pm) then SWITCH to AVOID LIGHT until 02:30 or later*

*TRAVELLING EAST: SEEK BRIGHT LIGHT between 12:30 and 15:30 (3:30pm) then SWITCH to AVOID LIGHT until 19:30 (7:30pm). On DAY 2 SEEK BRIGHT LIGHT between 15:30 (3:30pm) and 18:30 (6:30pm) then SWITCH to AVOID LIGHT until 22:30 (10:30pm)."*

***http://www.bodyclock.com***

To summarise...

- Change your eating and sleeping patterns, go to bed early and get up late (or vice-versa).

- Get plenty of sleep before your journey.

- Reduce alcohol intake.

- Don't eat more than usual.

# Nervous flyers

Http://www.airfraid.com offers a wealth of information for the nervous flyer, air travel remains the safest form of transport and this web site is extremely comprehensive. Various books covering this subject have also been published. The http://flyless.info web site provides information on alternative ways of travelling other than flying, http://www.seat61.com written by 'The Man in Seat Sixty-One' will tell you all about how to travel by train and ship.

> *"UK residents near Gatwick, Luton and Heathrow can take part in special fear of flying courses available from http://www.virtualaviation.co.uk on the internet."*
>
> **John, Gatwick**

To help with nerves...

- Distract yourself - occupy your mind by reading a book or listening to music.

- Sleep - try and get as much sleep as you can, the longer you're sleeping the less time you have to be nervous.

- Relax - wear an eye mask, recline your seat and imagine you are laying on a beach somewhere exotic.

- Tell the crew - Let them know you're a nervous flyer, they can help improve the flying experience for you.

## Personal hygiene

You'll be in a confined place for a long time and will sweat, feel sticky and be smelly. Use a long lasting antiperspirant deodorant before heading to the airport. You won't be allowed to take deodorant cans on aircraft so consider taking a roll on deodorant in your hand luggage. In situations of high security you might not be allowed any liquids or gels, including roll on deodorants.

> *I've witnessed a situation where an angry passenger was shouting at airport staff after he was gently advised that his personal hygiene was not suitable for air travel. To be frankly honest the airline had been very good and diplomatic about what was quite simply a horrible body odour and if I could smell it in the queue for check-in I'd hate to be the person sitting next to him for fifteen hours.*
>
> **Jim, London**

## Alcohol limits

Passengers under the influence of alcohol when checking in can be refused flight by the airline, so don't turn up drunk. Those who get drunk in the bar prior to the flight can also be refused flight when staggering to the gate. This can be a real nuisance to fellow passengers who can be delayed while the bags belonging to the paralytic passenger are searched for and removed from the aircraft. Alcohol is usually free on long haul flights, would you want to risk missing the flight by spending money to get drunk beforehand?

## Avoiding DVT (Deep Vein Thrombosis)

Http://www.airhealth.org is a good web site for finding all about this recent worry for air travellers. The web site states that around 3 to 5% of travellers will develop a clot, this apparently becomes evident a couple of days after the flight. Airhealth.org have an excellent page on DVT prevention which includes sections on leg flexing, compression hose, hydration and prophylaxis. The site also has a free printable pocket size leaflet for you to take with you.

> *"Deep Vein Thrombosis, or DVT, is a blood clot that can form in your legs and sometimes move to your lungs, where it could be fatal. In fact, complications from DVT blood clots contribute to more deaths each year than AIDS and breast cancer combined. And cancer and certain heart or respiratory diseases increase the risk. But the good news is, in most cases, DVT blood clots can be prevented."*

> ***http://www.dvt.net***

Walk around the plane a lot, getting plenty of exercise during the flight, but not during mealtimes.

> *"Drink a bottle of water every hour and your bladder will make sure you get up and walk about."*

> ***Gemma***

For even more information try searching for 'DVT' at http://www.bupa.com or visit the following site: http://www.dvt.net.

## Know the climate

Always be wary of the kind of weather and season you are about to fly in, pack appropriately for it. Some periods of the year are very hot, some destinations are unbearable to enjoy fully when the sun is giving it out big time. Remember that hot countries also have tropical storms, and a light-weight rain coat will be essential.

Read up on the weather in advance:

- http://weather.yahoo.com
- http://www.weather.com
- http://www.bbc.co.uk/weather/world

## Know the country

If you've always planned to explore New Zealand's beautiful countryside, check what season it is out there, it could be winter, have thick snow, ice and be very cold!

> *"I always go to http://www.wikipedia.org on the internet and search for the name of the country I'm visiting before I travel, and then read up about it."*
>
> *Jen*

Wikipedia is an interesting series of web pages, which are written by anybody and everybody, every page within the Wikipedia environment can be edited by you. It exists as an encyclopedia written by the man on the street and contains great amounts of information which has been collated over time. The people who write for Wikipedia also moderate Wikipedia, and that could include you too, it is everyone's job to question inaccurate facts and remove offending or inaccurate material. Wikipedia's first paragraph about Thailand, written in March 2006, was:

> *"The Kingdom of Thailand is a country in Southeast Asia, bordering Laos and Cambodia to the east, the Gulf of Thailand and Malaysia to the south, and the Andaman Sea and Myanmar to the west. Thailand is also known as Siam, which was the country's official name until May 11, 1949. The word Thai (???) means 'freedom' in the Thai*

*language and is also the name of the majority Thai ethnic group."*

**http://en.wikipedia.org/wiki/Thailand**

The article goes on to explain Thailand's history, politics, provinces (north, northeast, central, south, special governed districts), geography, economy, demographics, culture and miscellaneous information, including external links. The '???' reference in the text is an appeal from one Wikipedia author to others to revisit the sentence and back it up with evidence.

Http://www.justmaps.org is a great resource for world maps including a map showing where different languages are spoken, this is very useful. Http://www.hillmanwonders.com also contains a lot of useful information by Howard Hillman who has travelled to over 100 countries and has some very comprehensive impartial guides, my favourite being Canada (http://www.hillmanwonders.com/canada).

*"To find out the time right now in the country you're going to, check out http://www.timezonecheck.com online."*

**Mike**

# Beliefs and traditions

Always respect the culture you are visiting. Http://www.journeywoman.com/ccc is a good place for women to go to find out if there are any implications associated to wearing clothing in foreign locations, the site points out that wearing inappropriate clothing will affect safety, social interactions and can spoil an international visit.

General advice to women visiting Muslim countries is to cover legs and arms with comfortable clothing. Women should always cover hair in mosques; covering hair in public places can also help blend in. For travelling men I've learnt that clothing is less of an issue, although when working in Thailand I was advised to swap my shorts for trousers as a sign of respect to the people I was teaching.

*"I find http://www.sacred-destinations.com a useful place to start when researching my destination."*

**Jay**

*"If you are off to Japan read http://tinyurl.com/62shhz."*

***Pat***

# Medical jabs

The local doctors surgery or health centre will offer advice for the recommended vaccinations you will require prior to entering specific countries. Your travel insurance company may also require you to take some medical jabs before they grant your insurance policy.

When travelling to Thailand I was told that the jabs could take up to a month to take effect and that I should really have been injected at least six months previously. I took the decision not to have the injections, as I realised I'd be home before the protection would begin to work. The areas I visited were considered low risk, and I survived, but always explore the medical side of your trip well in advance.

Make an appointment with your doctor or local health centre well in advance to find out what you need, deal with it now if you've not already done so.

# Medicine

If you take set medication contact your doctor to ask if you need to alter the timed routine for taking medication during the journey to account for arrival in a new time zone.

Always pack enough of your medicine for your trip in its original packaging with clear dosage instructions and the contact details of your doctor. Pack enough to include any unforeseen delay which could bring you home later than you expected. If you use syringes for diabetes or other medical reasons check with your airline what their policy and documentation requirements are.

If you are travelling with a broken leg or arm ensure your doctor is aware and has provided you with pain medication adequate for the journey. Compression during flight can make a broken bone feel very uncomfortable and painful.

The http://www.dh.gov.uk/travellers web site by the UK Department of Health offers advice on how to get medical treatment abroad for UK citizens.

## Transporting medical drugs

If you are transporting medical drugs find out if you need to complete any paperwork. Countries such as the United States have strict rules, so consider taking medical certificates with you to support your case in the unlikely situation of difficulties.

> "Some countries, including the USA, have strict rules regarding the transportation of some medical drugs, even when a passenger is in transit between destinations."

> **Stella**

## Transporting illegal drugs

If somebody you do not know asks you to carry a bag for them at any point during your journey, don't. Passengers (even when in transit) found carrying illegal substances are severely punished. The penalty for carrying illegal drugs in Malaysia is death.

## Working abroad

Usually you'll fill out a visa application on the journey to your destination. If you plan to work in the country you are flying to you might need to fill out relevant work permits in advance. Check with your travel agent when booking, they might advise you to approach the embassy of the country you are planning to visit.

On arrival at your destination immigration officers may put you on the next plane home if they are unhappy with any aspect of your application.

> "If you are travelling to the United States always ask your travel agent about visa and documentation requirements."

> **Mark, London**

## Embassy

Have the contact details of your local embassy with you, if you lose your passport, or require emergency support, the embassy will be there to help you. Http://www.embassylist.com will provide you with the information you need.

*"For less popular tourist destinations consider registering with your embassy so they are aware that you are in the country."*

**Patrick R**

## Duty free, tax free and tariffs

Duty free in the United Kingdom refers to the liquor, tobacco and pure perfume that can be purchased (limits apply) within the airport or in flight on a journey, all other products purchased are therefore classed as 'tax free'.

When travelling from a country within the European Union into the United Kingdom you will not have to pay tax or duty on items you have bought from another member state of the European Union, so long as tax has been included in the purchase price. You must transport the goods yourself, and can give them as presents to other people, so long as a present does not substitute payment for other goods or services. Rules can and do change so check this information is still valid before you travel if you are a citizen of the UK.

All countries have a variation of similar rules on what they allow you to bring in, and take out of its borders. For UK residents, check out: http://customs.hmrc.gov.uk for a better idea of your rights and quantities of goods you can bring home.

*"If you are concerned that on your return to your homeland that a random search of your goods by customs suggests that things you took with you are believed to have been purchased abroad, then take copies of proof of purchase receipts with you when you travel. In on Asian country I was on an internal flight and proof my laptop was not bought there was needed to get past some tricky customs guys who were just doing their job, make it easy for them!"*

**Colin, Hull**

United States residents can register certain items with Customs and Border Protection (CBP) offices before they travel including cameras, watches, laptop computers, firearms, and CD players. Items must have serial numbers or other unique permanent markings, see if your country customs office offers the same service.

Firearms are not allowed in some countries or on most airlines. United States citizens; for more information visit the following web site: http://www.cbp.gov.

# Government advice

Being a British citizen I always check my government's 'Foreign and Commonwealth Office' information site at http://www.fco.gov. uk to discover what travel advice there is for British citizens visiting worldwide destinations.

The British, Foreign and Commonwealth office split countries into four sections:

- countries they advise against all travel to;

- countries where all travel to specific areas is not advised;

- countries they advise against all but essential travel to; and

- countries where all but essential travel to specific areas is not advised.

Justifications on the advice should be available to help you decide to take it, or ignore it. I'd take the advice if I were you. Different countries will have different reactions and opinions on each other. Opinions and advice will change and can be affected by factors such as natural disasters, government stability, and outbreaks of diseases until they are suitably contained or cured. Check out the official government web site for your country and explore the advice on travel to foreign regions.

# Car hire

Always take your full driving license documentation if planning to drive abroad. Basic understanding of the laws of driving, such as knowing which side of the road to drive on and localised road rules will be essential to getting around. When you arrive ask for advice from your hire car company or ask a local, they'll tell you how it is.

When hiring a car...

- Ask for a full explanation of the insurance policy attached to your hire contract and ask what the excess charge is if you crash the vehicle.

- Always return the vehicle with the same amount of fuel as when hired or you will be charged a penalty fee (unless a complementary tank of fuel is included).

- Ask what the charge is if you had the car for 25 hours, would they charge for two full days?

- The hire company usually charge extra if you plan to return the vehicle to a different location than it was collected from.

- If you plan to spend lots of time on the road only rent from companies that operate an 'unlimited mileage' policy rather than a rental price per mile. Some companies will give you an allocation of free miles, charging you per mile when you exceed the allocation.

- Good rental companies will give basic maps at no charge.

- Some companies will charge for extras, these include young drivers, additional drivers and the hiring of child seats, air conditioning, CD players and sunroofs.

If you have not pre-booked a hire car you might want to write down your hiring needs on a piece of paper while you're in flight, hey, you've got plenty of time! Duplicate what you've written down enough times to give each hire company a list of your needs on your arrival (you'll need about nine or ten copies, there a lots of hire companies to pick from). Distribute your hand written price requests to each of the hire companies' desk. Collect them from each company ten minutes later and compare what you've got.

> *"Note that the way dates are written can be different in other countries, eg November the 1st in the UK is written as 01/11/1955, however in the USA the same date is 11/01/1955, safer to write 01 November 1955 in this case."*

> **Malcolm**

# Rental Price Quote Request

Hire (date):                          from: _____ to: _____

Main driver:                                    _____

Date of birth:                                  _____

Nationality:                                    _____

Driving convictions: none / details:            _____

Additional driver:                              _____

Date of birth:                                  _____

Nationality:                                    _____

Driving convictions: none / details:            _____

Total number of people in vehicle:              _____

Anticipated mileage:                            _____

I am returning vehicle to:                      _____

Essentials (i.e. air conditioning/child seat):  _____

Please provide your best price for:

Small compact vehicle:                          _____

Medium sized vehicle:                           _____

Large vehicle:                                  _____

People carrier:                                 _____

Convertible:                                    _____

Damage excess cost:                             _____

Notes:


Please include tax in your quotation.

I'll be back in a few minutes to collect your quote.

I told the representative of a USA car hiring company that I was unhappy about having to pay $10 a day extra to include my brother as an additional driver, at twenty-four years old Andrew was one year younger than the age where adding drivers to the policy is free. I told the representative that Andrew is a safer driver than I am and surely it is unfair that I should be required to pay more money to drive less. In ten years on the road I've hit posts, trees, walls, fences and a pillar in a multi-story car park, Andrew has never hit anything. I explained that not adding my brother to the policy meant I would now not be upgrading the vehicle I had pre-booked and paid for. The representative automatically waived the $70 for my brother and upgraded the car to a larger vehicle for $70, he probably got great upgrade commission.

Another time at another American airport we contemplated how we would fit so much luggage in such a small car, before we knew it we had been upgraded for free for being a loyal regular repeat customer, all at the discretion of the manager.

> *"I knew someone who was refused car hire on arrival at his destination because he'd previously had a driving offence within the past five years! If you have any driving convictions check with the hire company before you travel!"*
>
> **Robert, Poole**

## Booking accommodation

If you are not planning on staying with cousin Shirley and her family, and you've not booked a package holiday, then you will need to consider where you plan to stay, and what the approximate cost per night will be. Travellers to the United States will need address details for their first night of accommodation to complete the check-in process at their arrival.

Http://www.laterooms.com is a useful web site for finding low cost hotel rooms around the world. I also advise you to use an internet search engine such as Google (http://www.google.com) or Yahoo (http://www.yahoo.com) to investigate the cost of local accommodation, you'll find that hundreds of hotels and bed and breakfast houses have their own web sites, and you will be able to contact them directly.

Sites worth a look include:

- http://www.hotelrooms.com

- http://www.hotelinfo.net

- http://www.lastminute.com/hotels

- http://www.hotels.com

or for the slightly more unusual night:

- http://www.unusualhotelsoftheworld.com

> *"Parrot Nest Lodge, Cayo, Belize: Thatched tree houses in Belize for starlight views in a woodland location. Parrot Nest is a truly unique tropical experience. Spending the night under a 100' guanacaste tree in a thatched tree house is like nothing else! The lodge is surrounded on three sides by the Mopan River, so a refreshing swim in clear water is never far away and the wildlife of the area abound. Yes, parrots are in great number here, along with hundreds of other types of birds, making this an ideal location for bird watching."*

**http://www.unusualhotelsoftheworld.com**

If it is the busy time of year you might have difficulty finding a hotel. I have a friend who turned up in a city thinking he would have no trouble finding a room for the night only to find thousands of people had descended on the city for an international convention of steam enthusiasts, finding a bed was a challenge!

Be aware that hotels are increasingly adding to fees that were once provided inclusive with room bookings, these potential extra charges include use of the gym, maid service, hospitality, early arrival fees, and additional charges for use of room service. If accommodation states 'resort fee' ask for information on what these additional charges are for when booking.

> *"When booking anything over the phone always take the name and direct telephone extension for the person you booked with. Always ask for a reference number."*

> **Kim**

On arrival visit the tourist information centre for help and advice booking local accommodation, including camping sites. Http:// www.hostelworld.com is a good site for backpackers travelling on a budget, you'll be able to book your beds online, but we wary about doing this unless you're happy to stick rigorously to your booked itinerary. Also consider the distances between hostels if you book a different one for every night, will you get there in time?

> *"Your hostel for the night will often phone the hostel at your next destination in advance to check availability and help book."*
>
> ### Carl, Bristol

Joining a hostel chain for a fee can provide discounted nightly charges and also reductions on other local amenities, attractions and restaurants. In England and Wales try the YHA (http://www.yha.org.uk). Http://www.hihostels.com and http://www.hostels.com are also worth a look.

With hostels, hotels, bed and breakfast and camping sites the general rule is the more nights you stay in one place the cheaper it gets.

If you're off to New Zealand, I've found that a great way to see the country is by road and camper van. Here are some hire companies:

- http://www.nzroadtrip.com

- http://www.campervanhirenz.co.nz

Http://www.motorhomebookers.com take bookings for Australia, Canada, Europe and the USA too. Compare the prices of lots of companies and always ask for a great deal.

> *"If you are planning a road trip across the USA this web page is a useful place to start: http://www.roadtripamerica. com."*
>
> ### John

How about meeting new people and sleeping on their couch? 'CouchSurfing' is an interesting project which offers couches around the world as beds for the night.

*"CouchSurfing is not about the furniture, not just about finding free accommodations around the world; it's about making connections worldwide. We make the world a better place by opening our homes, our hearts, and our lives. We open our minds and welcome the knowledge that cultural exchange makes available. We create deep and meaningful connections that cross oceans, continents and cultures. CouchSurfing wants to change not only the way we travel, but how we relate to the world!"*

**http://www.couchsurfing.com**

Those that like the idea of CouchSurfing might find the following interesting too...

- http://www.housecarers.com - contains details of house sitting opportunities.

- http://www.organicvolunteers.com - work for accommodation in farms, hotels and other places.

- http://www.globalfreeloaders.com - this is similar to CouchSurfing but you'll need to be prepared to host too.

- http://www.caretaker.org - another programme looking for people to look after their home rent free.

# Native tongue

Thai people are pleased when you attempt to speak their language with them, even the most basic of words. You'll earn more respect for trying than simply expecting the host nation to speak your language.

I always try to say the basic words, try and learn the following...

- Good morning/afternoon/evening.

- How are you today?

- Please and thank you.

- You are kind/helpful.

- Do you speak English?

'Khob Khun Kha' is how you say 'thank you' in Thai if you are a female, and 'Khob Khun Krab' is what you would say if you are male.

In learning new languages you will make mistakes, but trying is considered much more respectful than arriving at a destination and not knowing a single word. Your local college might offer a evening class introducing the language of the country you are planning to visit, phone them and ask.

> "Basic language books for most languages are available in most bookstores and the BBC'S Language site is excellent, find it at http://www.bbc.co.uk/languages online."

**Lorraine**

## Local emergency numbers

999 is the number you'll need to dial for emergency calls in the UK to connect to the Police, Fire, Ambulance services or the Coast Guard. Some countries have different numbers for the various services.

Here are some of the country numbers you might need:

| Country | Police Service | Ambulance Service | Fire Service |
|---------|----------------|-------------------|--------------|
| Argentina | 101 | 107 | 100 |
| Australia | 000 | 000 | 000 |
| Austria | 112 | 112 | 112 |
| Belgium | 101 | 100 | 100 |
| Brazil | 190 | 192 | 193 |
| Canada | 911 | 911 | 911 |
| Chile | 133 | 131 | 132 |
| Croatia | 92 | 94 | 93 |
| Denmark | 112 | 112 | 112 |
| Finland | 112 | 112 | 112 |
| France | 17 | 15 | 18 |
| Germany | 110 | 112 | 112 |

| Country | Police Service | Ambulance Service | Fire Service |
|---|---|---|---|
| Greece | 199 | 199 | 199 |
| Hungary | 07 | 04 | 05 |
| Iceland | 112 | 112 | 112 |
| Ireland | 999 | 999 | 999 |
| Israel | 100 | 101 | 102 |
| Italy | 113 | 113 | 113 |
| Jamaica | 119 | 110 | 110 |
| Japan | 110 | 119 | 119 |
| Kenya | 999 | 999 | 999 |
| Malaysia | 999 | 999 | 994 |
| Macedonia | 92 | 94 | 93 |
| Mexico | 08 | 08 | 08 |
| Netherlands | 112 | 112 | 112 |
| New Zealand | 111 | 111 | 111 |
| Norway | 112 | 113 | 110 |
| Poland | 997 | 999 | 998 |
| Portugal | 112 | 112 | 112 |
| Romania | 955 | 961 | 981 |
| Russia | 02 | 03 | 01 |
| Saudi Arabia | 999 | 997 | 998 |
| South Africa | 107 | 107 | 107 |
| Spain | 091 | 061 | 080 |
| Sweden | 112 | 112 | 112 |
| Switzerland | 112 | 112 | 112 |
| Taiwan | 110 | 119 | 119 |
| Thailand | 191 | | 199 |
| Turkey | 155 | 112 | 110 |
| United Kingdom | 999 | 999 | 999 |
| United States | 911 | 911 | 911 |

## Next of kin

Draw up a list of numbers in case of an emergency and store it with your documents, easily accessible around your person.

Fill in the < >'s...

---

### EMERGENCY / SOS

I am <name>, I am <nationality>.

I do/don't use any medication to support my health.

<details of medication>.

In emergency telephone my <relation> called <relation's name>.

Telephone mobile: <number, including international code> or home: <number, including international code>.

<relation> is in <country>.

---

Add other contact names and numbers in order that they should be phoned in an emergency. Attempt to translate the English version into the language of the country you are visiting on the back, use a phrase book, or ask the airline staff to support you if they are from the country you are going to.

Provide your contact number for friends and relatives to make contact with you. If you have access to the internet while away then regular use of email is a good way to stay in touch.

In some parts of the USA and UK there are campaigns suggesting that people list their emergency contacts in their mobile telephone address books as 'ICE' (In Case of Emergency), this helps emergency services call your designated next of kin much easier. Remember to prefix your 'ICE' numbers with the International dialling code for your home country.

## Phoning home

Calling from various telephones when abroad can be very difficult (prefix numbers complicate the process) if in doubt call the operator number on a public telephone (usually free and listed on the phone itself).

> *"Being a regular user of a mobile telephone, using the phone book feature makes me lazy, I no longer remember friends and family telephone numbers. I always carry a paper back up of important telephone numbers, I dread to think what would happen if I did not have that and lost my phone somewhere."*

**Nige**

# Using a mobile telephone abroad

Call your network provider to activate your mobile for international roaming if it has not already been activated, this can take up to two weeks to start working, some networks won't let you activate this service from your destination. Some networks will charge you for setting up this service.

Find out from your network provider how much calls will cost to dial home, send SMS messages home, and also how much you'll be charged if someone phones or texts while you are away.

Thoughts about mobiles...

- Check your model of phone will work on international networks.

- Usually a cheaper call rate abroad is a perk of a 'contract service' in comparison with a 'pay as you go' service.

- Sim cards and mobile phones can be rented at some international airports.

- Alter the numbers on your mobile phone to dial from abroad, for example a UK dialing code of 07777 would become 00 44 7777 (the first '0' is replaced with '0044')

- Add your country's local embassy number as a contact.

- Ask your network provider in advance how to access your answer phone messages in case there is no such service on arrival.

- It can be cheaper to buy a SIM card once you have arrived at your destination and use it in your existing handset. The following UK sites provide this service: http://www.uk2abroad.com and http://www.0044.co.uk.

• Pack the charger for your phone.

• You will probably need an adapter for foreign plug sockets.

• Write down your phone's unique serial number, its actual telephone number and the telephone number of your mobile operator. Keep this separate from your handset and use the information if your phone is lost or stolen to sort the problem out.

• Review your mobile phone contract and manual.

## Appear to be home

The friend, relative or neighbour who usually comes into your house and feeds the cat and waters your plants might also be on holiday when you plan to go away, so check their availability as soon as possible. Some pet kennels have limited space and get booked up early, enquire early if you need to.

Ensure your house looks lived in while away and nobody is home...

• Cancel milk and newspaper delivery.

• Consider asking a trusted neighbour to take in post and open and close curtains.

• Special plug socket timers that turn on and off lamps at certain times also help to make your home look occupied.

• Don't leave instructions in your house for your visitor to activate and deactivate your house alarm, train that person how to do it yourself.

*"Tell a nearby friend, family member or your neighbour when you are coming home and leave them some money to buy you some milk and bread so you won't have to travel far to get some, especially if the shops are closed."*

**Michelle**

Changing your answer phone message to say "I'm sorry, we're not able to take your call at the moment because we are out of the country" is not a good idea. Record something along the lines of "I'm sorry, we're unable to take your call right now, please leave a message and we'll get back to you soon."

*"If your neighbour has more than one car, could they park it on your drive while you are away? Mine does and it helps make the place look like someone is home."*

**Max**

## Settle commitments

Don't have any surprise letters awaiting you on your return; check you've paid bills with 'payment required by' dates. What about car insurance, home insurance, annual train travel passes and other things that might expire while you are away?

*"I once got back to my car at the long stay after three weeks abroad to find the tax disc had expired. I now check the disc before I travel."*

**Roger**

## Taking a pet

Little do people know how much easier it has become to take a pet with them on their travels. If you are a UK citizen, visit the following web site for detailed information about how to take your pet with you: http://www.defra.gov.uk/animalh/quarantine/PETS

An extract from the web page includes the following information:

*"The Pet Travel Scheme (PETS) is the system that allows pet dogs, cats and ferrets from certain countries to enter the UK without quarantine as long as they meet the rules. It also means that people in the UK can take their dogs, cats and ferrets to other European Union (EU) countries, and return with them to the UK. They can also, having taken their dogs, cats and ferrets to certain non-EU*

*countries, bring them back to the UK without the need for quarantine. The rules are to keep the UK free from rabies and certain other diseases."*

**Department for Environment, Food and Rural Affairs**
**http://www.defra.gov.uk**

The health of your animal is paramount and most animals, with the exception of some guide dogs will usually travel in the cargo hold of the plane. In the unlikely situation that I travel with my cat I'd ask her vet for advice. Some airlines will allow cats and dogs to travel in the cabin, check with your travel agent.

Most international airports will have an 'Animal Reception Centre' to check the health of all travelling animals. You'll have challenges checking pets into hotels and on some public transport, especially ferrets, probably.

Wikipedia has a great article on the Pets Passport Scheme with some good links to further reading: http://en.wikipedia.org/wiki/Pet_passport

## Travelling with babies, toddlers and children

A big challenge is to entertain younger travelling companions, they can get bored very easily on a flight if you don't prepare.

I remember one flight where a woman was boarding with a toddler, neither of them spoke English. As the plane hurtled along the runway and lifted into the air the toddler decided he was going to have some fun, leaving his seat he ran up and down the aeroplane, he was pretending to be an aeroplane himself as we slowly climbed up into the sky. I'll never forget that awful moment when he hurtled down the aisle to the back of the plane, screaming all the way. The boy's mother had no control over him for the duration of the twelve-hour flight, I was relieved to get off that plane.

*"At check-in ask for any buggy or pram you are taking to be stowed and returned to you as a 'priority', and you'll usually get the item back quite quickly once you have landed."*

**Sylvia**

Here are the best web sites I have found to get further advice for travelling with babies, toddlers and children:

- http://www.travellingwithchildren.co.uk

- http://www.flyingwithkids.com/travel_tips.htm

- http://www.holidaywithbaby.com

- http://www.takethefamily.com

One of these sites suggests audio story books are great for entertaining older children and can keep offspring happy for ages.

> *"For younger children take their favourite toys and introduce them one by one during the duration of the flight. Each time the child becomes restless swap the toy for another."*
>
> ### *Janice*

Flying out of Malaysia there was a woman sitting adjacent to me with a child who hated flying, he wanted to get off the plane. His mother very cleverly convinced her stressed child that the taxi of the aeroplane between the gate and the runway was the worst part of the journey, she congratulated him when the plane reached the runway ready for takeoff, the mother significantly calmed him down by emphasising that the worst part of the journey was over. The aeroplane then took off and the child was much calmer, fellow passengers smiled at each other in appreciation at the innovative thinking.

> *"Ask your travel agent at the booking stage about hire of cots, car seats and a buggy if you need them."*
>
> ### *Mummy JJ*

On another trip out of Atlanta International airport a mother pointed out to her child the off duty uniformed fire fighter sitting in the row behind her. The little boy was afraid of flying and stood on his chair for the entire duration of the flight (other than takeoff and landing), he was staring at the fireman as if he was some kind of superhero. The fire fighter pulled faces, played peek-a-boo, and dutifully sang in order to support the mother. Other passengers joined in with the song, it was really quite entertaining, my brother and I helped with the chorus, we were rubbish.

> *"Boeing 747's sometimes have baby fold out baby cots built into the seats, if you are travelling with a baby ask about this service."*
>
> **Darren, Hove**

Sarah Davey lives in Kent, is a Primary School Teacher and Mum to a two year old. Here are Sarah's first hand experiences of travel with a young child…

> *"Am I really insane? This was the question I kept asking myself over and over again before travelling with my daughter, Emma, on a holiday to the Gambia, West Africa. My friends thought I was completely mad and those with children of a similar age kept telling me how brave I was and that they'd never entertain the idea! However despite all reservations and sleepless nights of worrying (mainly caused by all the negative comments) we had a wonderful holiday and I'd definitely do it all again.*
>
> *We were lucky with our flight times and outbound was a 9am flight. This meant getting up reasonably early, to arrive at the airport to check-in at the earliest opportunity possible, before the crowds arrived. Travelling in the school Easter holidays meant the airport would be heaving and it paid to our advantage to check-in early as we didn't have to queue - definitely a first for me at London Gatwick!*
>
> *Being 13 months old, Emma was too big to use a sky cot and too young to have her own seat. When checking in we asked if the flight was full - it wasn't and an assistant kindly blocked out the seat next to me and my husband - giving us a whole row! This proved useful and I would even consider paying extra money in future to give the extra space needed for a toddler.*
>
> *I did have concerns over what she would eat on the aeroplane as Emma's always had a home made warm meal at lunch and dinner, if I ever gave her a sandwich to eat she'd be hungry an hour later! With this in mind and not being 100% sure over what customs would allow me through with, and how I could heat food in the air, I took a chance and packed a small cool bag with various*

*bits I knew Emma could snack on. I made a tuna pasta salad, some cheese sticks, carrot sticks, raisins, bananas and fromais frais (I just had to declare them as liquids and baby food whilst going through customs). I also had packed some 'just add water' baby breakfast porridges in case she wanted something hot. I ended up using these on the flight home for her dinner!*

*We'd packed her favourite straw cup and she drunk plenty of water. She drank loads during take off and landing, encouraged by us, and whether the sucking helped her ears or not we had no tears or evidence of pain - another success! Be warned the cabin pressure causes weird things - Emma's water beaker went mad squirting water everywhere!*

*Once through into the chaotic terminal we walked miles and miles around it - this was useful as Emma had boundless energy and we were keen for her to use it up in the hope she might pass out on the aeroplane. I think we walked the circuit so many times that I could probably name the shops in order! May I just add that yes Emma was walking strongly by the holiday after taking her first steps at 10 and a half months - we knew then we'd struggle to keep her sat still!*

*Depending on the airline, passengers with children are generally called on to the plane first as a priority (no such luck on our flight). I'd recommend getting on the plane first as this will ensure you claim room in the cabin luggage holds for all the extra baby paraphernalia you're carrying. The best thing I'd done was to pack a small toiletry bag with some nappies, a small pack of wipes, some perfumed nappy sacks, a thin fabric changing mat and some antibacterial hand gel. I could then quickly remove this from my bag and place it in the seat pocket in front of me so it was on hand when I needed it.*

*This leads me to the next all important concern of changing a nappy! When boarding the aeroplane find out where ALL baby changing toilets are (often a bigger changing table is at the rear of the aircraft) Believe me it'll be typical that when your little one fills their nappy that they'll be an air hostess trolley in the isle blocking the way you need to go. Not good if you have to wait, we all know the smell of a dirty nappy can waft, so by having an alternative you avoid this happening! The actual changing of your little one is an art form you'll master quickly. It's all good fun to have a squirmy, smelly bundle to hold while wrestling with lowering a change table in the tiny space of an aeroplane toilet!*

*Once on the aeroplane Emma was bemused as to what was going on but soon had to be secured to my husband's seat belt with an extra lap belt. This would have to remain until after takeoff, for any turbulence (luckily we had none - not sure how you'd get a sleeping child upright enough to get a lap belt round them and attached to yours!) and for landing. She hardly noticed for the first 20 seconds and then didn't want to sit still. Every distraction tactic was then deployed one after the other, watching the activities on the runway, playing peek-a-boo with the happy couple seated behind us, reading one of the six books packed into our hand luggage, playing with one of very few toys packed for the journey, playing with another, reading, playing and so on to keep her reasonably still and happy.*

*After takeoff she was able to use extra space to wriggle, move, stand, sit and continue with these activities occasionally going for a walk up or down the isle with Mummy or Daddy in tow, and sleeping for only one of the six hours! We weren't so lucky on our way home and a packed aeroplane meant no extra seat but being a night flight Emma passed out after her tea for 5 hours. This meant playing pass the sleeping baby as our arms and legs went dead after an hour! Despite all our worries Emma didn't cause as much agro as we thought she'd have and she was brilliant - surprising us totally. My husband had been practicing his 'I'm sorry, really sorry' routine for months before!*

*Now I have always found flights cold in the past and make sure I have lots of layers of clothes to remove when I arrive in the warmer destination. I applied the same rule to Emma, dressing her in comfy cotton leggings, vest and top. She was nice and cosy in these for sleeping, along with her blanket (stored in the buggy and just carried on the aeroplane) and her favourite cuddly toy ('Dog, Dog') who goes absolutely everywhere. Unlike me she was generally very hot and spent most of the flight there in just a vest, stripping down to just a nappy on arrival in Africa!*

*On arrival at your chosen destination don't believe your buggy will come off first - it doesn't! This can be very annoying as you try to keep a child safe in a busy terminal building with passengers crowding around the baggage reclaim. I found a quiet seat away from this area and allowed my husband to locate our bags while I carried on the entertaining. On return to London Gatwick the buggy arrived at a completely different belt to the luggage - something they don't tell you.*

*My last and final tip and the one that was most useful to us: take the Grandparents!"*

**Sarah Davey, Kent**

# Keeping in touch

The internet is a great place to gather information and now with blogging it has become an excellent place to tell the world what you are doing. Blogging is an online diary, millions of people all around the world keep blogs for both professional and personal reasons.

*"Rather than write emails home I now keep a travel blog which also publishes to my Facebook page, so my friends and family can read about the naughty things I've been up to while away."*

**Daniel**

Here are some places where you can get a free blog:

- http://www.blogger.com
- http://www.blog.co.uk
- http://www.typepad.com
- http://www.blogsource.com

- http://www.blogster.com

- http://www.wordpress.com

These listed services may place adverts on newly created blogs, you can usually pay a fee and have them removed if you want to.

> *"Friends and relatives can track the flight you are on and where it is in the world on sites such as http://www. flightstats.com, http://flightaware.com, and http://www. yahoo.com/travel - just tell them the flight codes."*

> **B. James**

'Myspace' has also become a popular place for people to write about themselves, and link their friends together. Once you set up a free MySpace you can invite friends and family to do the same. With MySpace you'll be able to keep your ramblings to your friendship group, rather than the wider world: http://www.myspace. com. 'Facebook' (http://www.facebook.com) and 'Bebo' (http://www. bebo.com) offer similar free services too, I find Facebook to be the best as it allows video and pictures to be uploaded and shared very easily.

> *"I make sure friends and family have a copy of my travel route including hotel phone numbers so in an emergency people can get in touch with me."*

> **Maxine, London**

Http://www.flickr.com and http://www.snapfish.com offer a free place to upload pictures to the net and share them. If you're an Apple Mac user check out http://www.mac.com and consider paying for a 'dot mac' account, it works well with your laptop if you are taking it with you. 'Dot mac' also makes online back ups of important stuff quickly an easily, essential in the horrible situation where a laptop is stolen.

> *"The video site http://www.youtube.com is good place to upload video files to for free and share with folks back home."*

> **Mitch**

*"My grandson Damian knows I'm not very good on this computer thing so he prints out his travel blogs when he is off travelling and sends them to me by post."*

**Granny Nat**

Letters and postcards sent home can take weeks to arrive, and for potentially worried relatives it is nice for them to receive a frequent phone call too.

*"To stay in touch with home I've found the http://www. netcafes.com web site useful to find the next internet café when travelling, http://www.world-newspapers.com is also useful to connect through to newspapers back home."*

**Geoffrey, Canada**

# Travel buddy

There are many subscription web site which will put travellers in touch with fellow travellers going to the same destination, the great thing about these sites is they let you review potential travellers' profiles, and find out a bit about them before making contact.

Don't send any money to someone who wants to be your travel buddy and ensure you are in control of your own booking arrangements.

Some buddy sites:

- http://www.travelmatesonline.com

- http://www.travellersmeet.com

- http://www.companions2travel.co.uk

*"If you are planning a trip and don't want to go alone consider writing to your local newspaper or contacting a local radio station to put an appeal out for a travel buddy, a short appeal on the radio and I found Cheryl, we get married next September."*

**Jack, Newcastle**

## Web check-in

As this chapter comes to a close it is worth mentioning that some airlines allow travellers to check-in for a flight in advance of arriving at the airport. Travellers with absolutely no hold luggage that have plans to purchase clothing and suitcases abroad (usually at reduced rates) might enjoy this time saving experience. Check with your airline web site to see if this service is useful to you.

> *"I always prepare the clothing I want to wear for the journey to the airport and trip on the plane ready for when I wake up in the morning of departure. I also make sure I have a clean set of clothes ready for when I get back so I can shower and change quickly before tackling the cases full of dirty washing."*

> *Joan*

## New security measures for the USA

The USA have now introduced their 'Electronic System for Travel Authorisation' (ESTA).

US Customs & Border Control have introduced the system as web based only, it requires all passengers (including infants) travelling **to** or **via** the USA to apply for 'authority to travel' a minimum of 72 hours prior to travel. This procedure is effective from 12 January 2009 and is compulsory. If you are flying to or through the USA ask your booking agent about ESTA.

British passport holders (other nationalities check with your booking agent) travelling to or via the USA are required to have either individual **machine-readable** passports or **biometric passports**. Families will be required to obtain individual passports for each traveller including all children.

British citizens will benefit from carefully reading information on the US Embassy (http://www.usembassy.org.uk) web site.

# 3

# Packing

*"For my part, I travel not to go anywhere, but to go. I travel for travel's sake. The great affair is to move."*
*Robert Louis Stevenson (1850 - 1894)*

## Pack what you actually need

For an international flight you'll generally be allowed about 20kgs per person, but probably 30kgs if you're flying business or first class (each airline varies). I try and pack no more than 15kgs and this gives plenty or room to bring back souvenirs and gifts.

> *"Watching a documentary some time ago the star of one episode was a British television legend on board a cruise ship. To reduce luggage the celebrity apparently washes his boxer shorts every evening before going to bed ready to reuse them the following day. If you can get clothing dry in time, this actually makes good sense and I find that the towel warmer in a hotel room is great for drying my pants."*
>
> *Paul K*

The 'Universal Packing List' can be found at http://upl.codeq. info and has been online since 1993. The site will ask a series of questions which will then generate a custom packing list for you, it'll even email you the list. The http://www.onebag.com web site is also a great resource for the art of travelling light, check out the links page on the site for further reading.

*"Take wrapping paper and sticky tape with you in your case if you plan on presenting gifts to others on your journey. I once had gifts I'd carefully wrapped up for a wedding opened by customs in a random security check."*

**Donna, Denmark**

## Picking a suitable suitcase

If great Auntie Elsie offers to lend you the suitcase that once belonged to Great Uncle Wilfred then politely decline. Apart from having somebody else's suitcase to protect for your trip it will probably be far too old and impractical for modern air travel.

*"You'll either need to pick a suitcase or a backpack that is ripe and ready to be your best friend for the duration of your trip, pick the wrong one and you'll regret it."*

**Alex**

I saw what I thought was a great deal on a suitcase in a clothing store. I remember thinking at the time that it was a strange place to find a suitcase for sale, but it was a bargain, looked durable and it had plenty of sections and pockets. It was the only size suitcase they had on sale and it looked pretty big, I pondered for a moment, thought about it, then bought it. Big mistake. I should have thought much harder, why was a clothing chain selling a suitcase range in just one size?

I was so proud when I walked through the doors to the airport, my great new suitcase following behind obediently with ample space to store anything I decided to buy on my journey. When I got to the queue for check-in and stood my shiny new suitcase upright I discovered just how huge it was. Being the only case in the clothing store, I had no other brands to compare it with, had I known, I'd never bought it.

Obviously, the clothing chain's buyer had been offered a great deal on some suitcases by a luggage wholesaler with loads of oversize cases they could not shift. The clothing store then sold on what they advertised as a great bargain to their unsuspecting customers who could not resist a great deal (and were really in their store to purchase pants and socks). So when purchasing something, I've learnt to buy from a place which has comparative goods for sale.

*"Start packing at least five days before your departure, you'll end up compiling a list of things you'll need to borrow or buy and still have plenty of time to get them. Packing on the night before a trip is not a good idea."*

**Jemma, Liverpool**

Ultimately, this was one of the most embarrassing things I've ever experienced when travelling on an international trip. Bus drivers complained because it was awkward to stow in the luggage compartment, the airline check-in girl frowned as she saw just how gigantic this case was, as I was struggling to get it across her scales, the hotel porter asked me where my wife and kids were, and made noises implying they were in the case. The case was awkward to store at every place I stayed, and even worse I had problems fitting it in cars. I never used that case ever again.

*"When buying a case, buy something which you know will fit your clothing and will have space or can be expanded to carry any excess goods you've bought."*

**Raymond**

*"Get a good padlock, but be aware that customs officers in some countries will break the padlock off if they want to look inside to check that the contents are legitimate, they won't replace it."*

**Gemma**

*"To make my case distinctive I've got some REALLY GAUDY strips of fabric (off cuts from a market stall) that I tie round the handles of my case. It is without doubt, if I say so myself, a BRILLIANT thing to do to make your life a heck of a lot easier."*

**Drew, UK**

Cases with wheels are a great idea (big wheels, not tiny ones). You'll be dragging your case on all kinds of surfaces including car parking areas, bumping up kerbs, across gravel and other uneven surfaces. Insist on big, durable wheels.

*"When packing the case remember that when you tow it behind you it will be almost horizontal so pack the heavier items, such as your shoes, near the wheels. If you have difficulty towing a case, try pushing it, this could be easier."*

**Rebecca**

Selecting a distinctive suitcase is a great idea, try and buy one that stands out, or that you can customise so that when you are standing next to the luggage belt you can identify yours quickly and easily.

Thoughts...

- How flexible is your suitcase for the amount of stuff you plan to take?

- How mobile are you with your luggage, especially if travelling alone? If you can't manage, cut down what you're taking.

- How durable is the case? If it is old and well travelled, is it likely to split open?

- You'll probably bring back more things than you take with you, will there be enough space for a busy case on the return journey?

*"When flying out of an airport in Florida both my wife and I were charged $20 per kilo that our suitcases were overweight. The airline were strict with a 20 kilo allowance per suitcase and fined us $240 in total. I thought we were allowed 30 kilos each and we are very careful with our weight limits now."*

**Mark**

*"Extra straps to wrap around your case and give it extra protection from bursting open are a good buy, and they help to distinguish luggage from others, you can even get them customised with your name."*

**Mike R**

If anyone wants to buy a suitcase, I have one for sale.

# Selecting the right backpack

Not all globetrotters will travel with a suitcase, some will need to travel light and take their accommodation with them. If planning to go on a trip where you'll be sleeping under the stars and eating out of saucepans think twice before you pack a gas canister for a cooking stove.

*"Most backpacks are made from a durable nylon material and are very durable to sustain the elements. Despite this, whenever I go on a hike with a big backpack I always line it with a thick refuse sack to add extra protection from the weather."*

**Dartmoor Letterboxer**

*"Try on lots of backpacks, the general rule is the more expensive the product, the better it actually is."*

**Ben**

*"If you are packing more than 26lbs (12 kg) consider a backpack with a padded hip belt... hips, rather than shoulders will support most of the load."*

**Tac Tic**

In New Zealand I visited an 'outdoors store' to buy a backpack for a short excursion to Queensland on the South Island. I really needed something that would contain essentials for three days and could be carried on my back. On inspecting the various options, I failed to find one that was the size that could be compacted in order to fit in my suitcase for the remainder of the trip. Talking to the sales staff they pointed me to the 'discontinued sales items', I found many backpacks at significantly reduced prices simply because they were 'last years line', I snapped up a bargain.

*"I pack as little clothing as possible knowing I'll buy clothes as I travel usually at either half or a third of the price they cost here."*

**Yan, London**

## Hand luggage

Economy passengers are usually allowed only one item of hand luggage each, business class passengers will usually find they can take two. Airlines have different policies regarding hand luggage allocation, check with your booking agent as to what you are allowed.

*"I always pack my slippers in my hand luggage and change into them during the flight."*

**Sylvia**

At a London airport I witnessed a passenger arguing with UK security over her video camera bag. In her opinion the video camera bag was not a second item of hand luggage, it clearly was. At the same airport a very distressed Canadian lady was most annoyed to be refused through the security area because she had a hand bag and a rucksack, she was in tears as both were packed to the brim and she had to start throwing personal belongings in the bin, her suitcase had already been checked for the flight.

*"Suitcases are often loaded onto the conveyor belts at airports with their wheels facing upwards, if you have any pockets on the front I'd avoid filling them with breakable items."*

**Anon**

Hand luggage allocation will also include any duty free goods bought at the airport, ensure you leave enough space to carry any purchases you anticipate making. If two of you are travelling together try and share one bag to take on the plane and use the other bag for duty free.

Here are what some would consider as hand luggage essentials:

- passport;
- full driving license (card and paper if new style UK);
- identification;
- other forms of identification;
- visa (where applicable);

- international vaccination documents (if needed);

- health and travel insurance documents;

- itinerary (including flight numbers);

- travel documents (tickets, reservations, onward transportation);

- currency (credit cards, travellers cheques, small change);

- list of all belongings;

- toiletries (absolutely no aerosol cans);

- tissues;

- camera equipment (batteries, charger and tapes);

- original packaged medication (travel sickness pills);

- reading material;

- music player and headphones;

- flight socks (surgical stockings or ladies tights!);

- comfortable pillow (inflatable);

- spare glasses, sun glasses;

- underwear (change at the transit airport half way);

- pen and note pad (you'll need the pen to fill out a landing card);

- bottle of water for the flight (liquids are sometimes not allowed in hand luggage);

- breath mints.

> *"Pack food in your hand luggage to eat at the Airport. Airport food is typically more expensive, especially bottled water."*
>
> ***Marc***

Consider adding to your hand luggage a set of noise reduction headphones. This type of headset will work with your music player and will listen to the sounds of the space around you and cancel out noise. You don't need to listen to music, use the headset to simply remove cabin noise.

*"Fill your mp3 player with some podcasts as well as your favourite music to pass the time."*

**Anon**

For reasons of security do not carry any sharp items including knives, letter openers, scissors, tweezers, cutlery and nail files. Sports bats, snooker cues, knitting needles and darts are also not allowed.

If you're taking your laptop with you make it an easy job to get it in and out of your hand luggage. Customs at some countries require it to be placed separately in a tray when it goes through the scanner.

*"My ten year old is kept happy for hours by playing with his handheld games console. I always make sure he has plenty of puzzle games to play as they occupy his mind and also tire him out."*

**Michelle**

During increased levels of security hand luggage restrictions can be restricted further below the size and weight limitations, check with the airline to find out the current limitations. Liquids and gels can also be banned from hand luggage.

*"I've seen very distressed female passengers parting with very expensive perfumes because they have not followed the rules."*

**Bill**

## First aid kit

Sharp first aid items are not allowed in hand luggage during air travel, ensure your first aid kit is stowed safely and well protected within a suitcase or backpack.

First aid essentials could include:

- first aid manual;
- headache tablets;

- sterile bandage;

- plasters;

- scissors;

- tweezers;

- sterile bandage;

- antibiotic ointment;

- antiseptic wipes;

- eye wash;

- thermometer;

- emergency prescribed medication.

You might also consider antihistamines, allergy medication, nausea medication and ibuprofen.

## Backpack Essentials

Here are some essentials worth considering if you are planning on going on a trip which will require a backpack:

- toothbrush;

- toothpaste;

- washcloth;

- towel;

- swim wear;

- deodorant;

- soap;

- shampoo;

- lightweight raincoat;

- cooking utensils;

- sun screen;

- after sun;

- sun hat;

- warm hat;

- gloves;

- first aid kit;

- tissue paper (if you decide to use nature's leaves watch out for stinging nettles and poison ivy);

- cork screw;

- bottle opener;

- can opener;

- flask;

- water bottle;

- plastic cutlery, cup and plate;

- bug repellant;

- sleeping bag;

- tent;

- torch;

- spare torch batteries;

- mobile phone charger;

- gifts for hosts;

- clothing, suitable for the climate and duration of the trip.

*Some hostels rent you a sleeping bag and pillow at an extra charge and cooking utensils are usually available for use at hostels. Buy safety matches at your destination, don't pack any flammable items as airport staff will confiscate it and won't help you repack your bag once they have found it!"*

**Glenn**

# Packing a backpack

*"Pack a Backpack?! Well, I packed nicely the first time, all items folded and not creased... however that philosophy went straight out of the window, as within 2 days of being on the trip (in New York), I busted one of the side zips because I tried to stuff too many boxers and socks in one pocket! From that day forth, it was a case of 'if it don't fit, it ain't going!'*

*Packed to the rafters was an understatement, but I took 14 t-shirts with me, along with 2 weeks worth of underwear... Stupid idea, I must admit but being away for a year, I wanted lots of choice, as I knew I'd get bored with all my clothes... however, the 'phantom sock thief' did strike on several occasions, only to leave me desperately short! Fortunately my parents brought me over some replenishments. My armour was back up and 100% fully operational. We'd gone for a year but I'd packed for life!*

*Pack a backpack similar to a suitcase; shirts on top to avoid them creasing; t-shirts possibly just underneath and the things you need to get to quickly always toward the top. However, it came to a point when you're forced to check out of a hostel at 10am, and it's 09.45, you're hung-over, bleary-eyed and simply throw it all in and hope it fastens up, and all this to the theme tune to the Benny Hill TV show."*

**Richard Pont**

There are also some great little movies on You Tube about packing including:

 • pack for a hiking day trip - http://tinyurl.com/3drcdf

 • how to roll up a sleeping bag - http://tinyurl.com/2ua3jj

Backpackers will also benefit from taking a look at the http://artoftravel.com web site and also http://www.backpackeurope.com for further tips and advice.

*"Always check baggage allowance in advance, I went over by a few kilos and was fined by the airline."*

**Ray T**

## Packing a suitcase

An ideal suitcase will arrive at your destination undamaged with everything inside intact and wrinkle free. Pack the right clothing for the climate and consider what you'll need for the duration of the journey.

If you can wash clothing at the hotel, do it. If you can cut down on the amount of clothing you take, do it.

*"The absolute top tip for packing for more than one person is to share suitcase space. If you're travelling with friends and family pack some of your clothing in their cases. If you're travelling with a partner pack half your stuff in their case and half theirs in yours, if a case goes missing you'll still have clothing to wear. It is no good simply packing all your underwear in one case and shirts in another, you'll need to balance your bits out evenly."*

**Lisa**

Packing tips...

- Pack only essentials you know you are going to wear.

- Write down activities (swimming, horse riding, dining out) you plan to take part in and what you need for that activity.

- Estimate where and when you'll be able to wash your clothing (if at all) during your trip and pack enough to get you to that moment.

- Try on all clothes you've put away especially for the trip, see if they fit and if you can visualise yourself wearing them at your destination.

- Write down everything you pack and when you come back mark all the items you did not use.

- On your return write the items you had to buy or forgot (store these notes in the suitcase ready for next time).

*"If you're currently in the summer season and travelling to the winter don't pack your coat in your suitcase, it will take up too much space. Wear your coat onto the plane and hand it to the air steward or stewardess and they will hang it up for you, obviously try not to forget it when you*

*arrive at the destination airport.*

*When flying from winter to summer you might need your coat on the way to the airport and on the way home from the airport. If you've arranged a lift for your airport journeys then ask that person to take your coat home and bring it back for you on your return."*

**Sal**

Consider the following as potential suitcase essentials for your journey:

- toiletry bag (including toothbrush, toothpaste, washcloth, soap, shampoo, deodorant, shaving razors and foam);

- emergency toilet roll;

- swim wear (small towel for the beach);

- flip flops;

- bug repellant;

- sun cream;

- after sun;

- sun hat or warm hat;

- plug adapter;

- mobile phone charger;

- reading material;

- your favourite brand of tea/coffee;

- more home comforts (within reason);

- presents (for people you stay with);

- enough clothing to suit the climate;

- corkscrew (taking a bottle of wine back to your hotel room is cheaper than drinking from the mini-bar);

- swiss army knife (can be a cork screw and can opener too).

As a reminder, the last two items should not be put into your hand luggage, as they would be confiscated.

Things that should not be put in the suitcase or a backpack for flight include:

- cigarette lighters;
- fuel;
- matches;
- chemicals;
- paint (and thinners);
- camping gas;
- fuel blocks;
- fireworks;
- compressed gas cylinders;
- ammunition.

> *"The night before I travel I always lay out the clothing I'm planning to wear for the next day for my journey. My suitcase is always fully packed, and closed up. I also make sure I've got a razor, toothbrush and toothpaste available other than the ones buried deep in my wash bag in the middle of my case. On my return journey I usually use and then abandon my holiday toiletries in the hotel room before heading to the airport."*
>
> **Daniel, Perth**

Rolling clothing while it is still warm from the dryer will help to stop wrinkles, also laying tissue paper between clothing items will have the same effect. I pack as many breakable items as possible in shoes wrapped in clothing. Never pack a breakable item near the edge of a case.

> *"I never put copies of important documents in my suitcase. What if the case was to get lost or be delayed? I always photocopy all my important documents and carry them with me; I leave the originals, including my passport in the hotel safe."*
>
> **Steven**

I put the heavy stuff, such as shoes, jeans and jackets at the end of the case with the wheels. The lighter stuff I pack at the non-wheel end and this all contributes to making moving about easier. I put footwear in plastic bags to avoid any dirt getting on clothing and always ensure I take footwear with me which I've worn before and know won't hurt my feet.

> *"When my mother packs she'll leave enough space to squash in her favourite pillow from her bed, helping her to have a comfortable night in foreign hotel rooms."*
>
> **Ben**

> *"I weigh my suitcase on the bathroom scales to check I've not gone over the weight limit."*
>
> **Joy**

If you are flying to the USA always check the following web page for advice on permitted and prohibited items: http://tinyurl.com/ptxdw.

> *"Give the spare key for your case to your travel partner to look after."*
>
> **Gregg, Leicester**

For even more help packing a suitcase go here: http://daisy.co.nz/travel/how-to-pack-a-suitcase

Or even the way butlers do it:

- Youtube video part 1: http://tinyurl.com/2ock3m

- Youtube video part 2: http://tinyurl.com/2l9gy2

> *"Buy plug adapters in supermarkets and DIY shops rather than paying top dollar at the airport."*
>
> **Matt**

## What to wear

- Dress for a long haul flight is typically 'smart casual'.

- Wear comfortable and roomy items.

- Pick comfortable and clean footwear that has been worn before.

- Wear a comfortable jumper or pullover onto the plane, take it off and use it to make yourself more comfortable (I use mine as a make-do pillow) during the flight.

- Feet can expand as much as one shoe size while in flight so be conscious that if you take your shoes off they might not fit back on again for a short period.

- Consider other passengers when applying perfumes.

- Use an antiperspirant rather than a deodorant.

> *"I always 'break in' new shoes by wearing them at home for a few hours each evening before travelling, this means I don't get blistered uncomfortable feet the first time I wear them abroad all day long."*
>
> **Gerome**

> *"Low cabin pressure can cause the body to swell slightly, so the choice of wardrobe for a flight is essential when it comes to comfort. Pick clothing that doesn't feel restrictive when seated and accommodates for bloating."*
>
> **Ben**

# 4

# Airport

**"When everything seems to be going against you, remember the airplane takes off against the wind, not with it."**
*Henry Ford (1863 - 1947)*

## Alarm call

If you are booked on an early morning flight be sure you've prepared everything you need the night before and checked your alarm clock is working properly, if you have alternative alarms set them too.

When getting a lift to the airport from someone who does not live in your house ask if they would like you to telephone to be their wake up call. Consider putting your alarm clock well away from bed, so you can't just turn it off and go back to sleep. If you are staying in a hotel the night before you travel you will be able to book a wake up call at reception.

> *"If travelling to the airport in early morning the roads should be relatively trouble free, but be aware of rush hour traffic as commuters wake up to congest matters."*
>
> *Jeff*

When travelling by public transport be sure you know the timetables and have planned carefully to arrive at the airport in plenty of time. Most public transport operators will operate a varied timetable during weekends and public holidays. Book tickets in advance.

If you plan on using a taxi firm; telephone local companies and ask for quotes, also telephone taxi companies nearer the airport for comparisons.

> *"Be strict on the actual time you plan to depart your home for the airport, make sure everyone involved knows, especially the taxi company you are using."*
>
> **Paul, Walthamstow**

## Loading the car

I carry my life around in my car, the 'boot' (Americans read as 'trunk') is always full with too much junk, and many an airport run I've frantically had to empty it all out to make room for luggage. Be sure you've got plenty of boot space for you cases. Bend your knees and keep your back straight as you lift heavy luggage in with care.

> *"Both my wife and I assumed each other had put the suitcases in the car boot, we discovered our error on arrival in the long stay parking area at the airport."*
>
> **James**

## Before departing

- Double check you have all your documentation, passports and tickets.

- Lock all windows and doors.

- Unplug electrical items.

- Throw away any food that could go off in the fridge.

- Do whatever you usually do with your heating/water supplies while away (turn down or off).

## Journey to the airport

- If in the UK tune into the local BBC station for the county you are passing through for regular travel news.

- Have the airline telephone number to hand in case you need to call them.

  *"Some mobile communications companies offer on demand travel information by dialing a special number, find out if your mobile company offers this service, it could tell you just how long you'll be stuck in traffic for."*

  **Pete**

# Parking

Often more than one company offer long stay parking at the airport, if you have booked in advance make sure you arrive at the right parking area. If you have not booked in advance some parking areas will allow you to use a personal credit card as a ticket, recording your entry time and exit time, also charging the final bill to the same card.

  *"I leave drinks and food in the vehicle for my return journey, just in case I did not fancy the flight food and feel hungry for something familiar. I also park my car as close to the airport carpark bus stop as possible so dragging luggage between car and bus is an easy job."*

  **Jan**

A frequent transfer bus will arrive and take you from distant parking areas to the airport terminal. If the bus takes a long time to turn up that should not really matter as you've factored in plenty of time to get to the terminal!

Parking tips...

- Ensure you park in the right parking area, for the car parking company you booked with (short, medium or long term).

- Park in a designated space, or risk your vehicle being towed.

- Take the parking ticket with you, don't leave in the car unless it states to do so.

- Lost tickets will usually result in a charge for a maximum stay fixed penalty.

- Remove all valuables from view in the vehicle.

- Write on the parking ticket the zone your car is parked in, if you don't have a pen use your camera phone or digital camera to take a picture of the car parking location sign. If children are travelling with you ask them to remember the location, they wont forget.

> *"I used satellite navigation (satnav) to get to the airport, I parked up in the long stay removed the unit from the windscreen before putting it in my bag. I returned to the vehicle two weeks later to find someone had tried to break in. The Police told me even though I'd done right by not leaving the satnav in the car there was a mark on the inside of the windscreen, where the attachment had been stuck; this apparently is a sign to thieves that a satnav unit could be in the vehicle. I always clean off the mark now everywhere I go."*
>
> ***Ronald***

## Arriving at the terminal

At busy international airport security staff are usually outside the airport ensuring cars don't stay too long while dropping off passengers. The specially provided drop off zones are designed to cope with a fast turnover of people arriving so if friends or family are dropping you at the airport make your goodbye with them a quick one. The person that drops you off will not be able to help you into the terminal, as they can't leave their car unattended.

Once you're outside the airport collect a trolley to help transport your luggage to the check-in desk, trolleys are usually free but at some countries you'll have to use a coin. If you or one of your party has a disability ask for assistance from airport staff, who will know where wheelchairs and transport support is available.

Don't leave your baggage while you get a trolley, never leave your luggage unattended.

## Entering the airport

As soon as you enter you will be faced by screens giving you flight numbers with the location of the corresponding check-in desks where you can now head to and part with your luggage. Never leave your luggage with strangers who could tamper with it. If you see unattended luggage report it immediately to the nearest airport staff and move well away from it.

The airport can be a very busy place so be aware at all times of other passengers moving around you. Try not to block other people by stopping in busy walkways. Please don't lay across three or four seats, making other people stand, I might be one of those who is shattered too and needs a sit down.

> *"London Gatwick airport 'South Terminal' has some special near vertical relaxing seats, you'll find them underneath the escalator which goes up to the food court."*
>
> **Mike**

# Check-in

Katy Wills works as a 'Passenger Service Agent' at London's Stansted Airport.

> *"Stansted is the third busiest airport in the UK. With 30 airlines serving over 170 destinations, and over 22 million passengers passing through the airport, many leading low-cost scheduled airlines have made Stansted their base."*
>
> **http://www.stanstedairport.com**

You'll usually find Katy checking you in for your flight, and she has some information which will help us all to get away from check-in and through to duty free as quickly and easily as possible...

> *"We get all kinds of interesting and strange requests on the check-in desks, most recently I was asked by a lady not to seat her next to any another female on the flight. Expired passports are a regular occurrence, only the other day I had to explain to a passenger why a passport would have an expiry date and no matter what he thought about it, I was unable to check-in someone who's passport was three years out of date. Needless to say he did not fly that*

*day and his girlfriend was not very pleased with him.*

*When arriving at the airport be sure that you line up at the right desk, it's amazing how many people wait in line for completely the wrong flight and have to go and queue up again somewhere else!*

*Once you're in the right line make sure that you:*

- *have your passport and tickets to hand;*

- *know the city you are flying to, it helps me process you faster than when you tell me the country name, or say 'I don't know, my assistant booked it';*

- *decide if you want a seat by a window or aisle (if you've not pre-booked a specific seat); and then*

- *do a final check to ensure you're carry on and hold luggage is tagged with the address of the final destination.*

*I'll ask you security questions, which you should answer honesty and truthfully. Watch your luggage at all times and do not let anyone interfere with your belongings or accept any goods from strangers who have asked you to carry goods for them. If you are approached, contact airport securities immediately, do not put yourself at risk.*

*Passengers get refused flights for all manners of reasons, including the classic 'passport expired' situation along with being drunk, abusive, turning up to the check-in desk after the flight is closed and the rather strange passengers who joke about having bombs, guns or drugs in their bags. Even when passengers joke we have to take it seriously, the fines issued by higher authorities can be up to £5000 and seven years in prison for responses that put others at risk.*

*I'll soon tell you if your luggage is overweight and might have to charge you an excess baggage fee, its always advisable to check your ticket before you travel, it should have the weight allocation you are allowed for travel on your flight. If you're hand luggage is too big, I'll have to check it into the hold, so please be careful when you pack that you meet requirements.*

*We're wise to every passenger trying to get the seats with the leg space, so don't think you're the first who has asked today! There are emergency seats which do have ample leg room, but due to them being located next to a working emergency door, are not available for people under the age of 16, disabled, pregnant, infants, obese, the elderly and nervous flyers. Deportees and prisoners are also not allowed to sit in those seats when flying with the airline I work for. Different airlines will have different policies as to who can sit in the emergency door seats, if you are tall and think you're physically able to support the crew during an emergency by helping other passengers out of the emergency door, then there is no harm in asking. People suffering from back, neck and leg problems, I'm sorry, but you'll probably be declined an emergency exit seat. It also pays to be nice, polite and happy when asking for that special seat!*

*Listen carefully when we provide you with your ticket, seat number and details of the departure time, we'll be able to point you in the direction of the gate, please don't be late for the boarding of the plane as it really causes yourself and fellow passengers problems. Watch out for the screens dotted around the terminal, they'll tell you when boarding has commenced, its best to be standing near the gate when boarding is called rather than running.*

*If you are travelling by the same airline on more than one plane to your destination then I will probably issue you with your boarding card for the second flight of your journey too, keep it safe. The return journey boarding card will be issued on your return journey when you check-in at your departure airport.*

*Working on a check-in desk is really quite demanding, every day is different and I really enjoy meeting most travellers. I've checked in football managers, TV personalities and Royalty, same rules apply to everyone.*

*We're always ready and willing to help you where we can*

*and look forward to welcoming you to your airline.*

*Enjoy your flight and keep your passport, boarding card and documents safe at all times."*

**Katy Wills**

Once you've been checked in and parted with your baggage you'll head off through the security checks. As you go through security your recently checked-in hold luggage will also be scanned to ensure that the contents are safe for travel in the aircraft, if you are carrying something in your suitcase which should not be there expect to be challenged when you reach the departure gate.

*"When trying for leg space you make yourself as tall as possible, don't slouch. Stand up straight, stand on tip-toes if you can and be as broad as possible. I think the airline will have at least six banks of three seats which they will reserve for the tallest travellers, ensure you complement the check-in staff, be friendly, ask them how their day is and smile."*

**Tall Guy**

*"I've found that some of the front row economy seats are now being sold by airlines at a higher rate because of the ample legroom, they call these seats 'Premium Economy'."*

**Amanda**

*"Get a window seat if you want to rest your head against the window and have a sleep."*

**Jane**

## DIY check-in

Do-it-yourself check-in is a recent evolution. Some airlines, including British Airways and Virgin allow passengers to check-in for a flight at an 'express check-in computer terminal' in the airport, or by logging onto the internet at home. Checking in early has some great advantages, including the ability to pick seats on an interactive aircraft plan. Some flights are not eligible, the nearby airline representative will be able to help you.

Once you've completed the procedure and you've collected any documentation or boarding pass that the terminal has printed for you head to the 'express bag drop' and part with your luggage. If you've not received a boarding pass from the 'express check-in terminal' you'll get it from the person taking your luggage.

# Upgrade

Katy tells me that the airline she works for looks for frequent flyers amongst their economy passengers for upgrade to business class when economy is overbooked. A good frequent flyer community exists at http://flyertalk.com online.

Graham Hart of Chelmsford has a different experience:

*"I cannot guarantee that this will work, but it has for me more than once particularly on long haul. Upgrades usually occur when there is over-booking in lower class and space in business class. But how do they choose whom to upgrade? The key for the airline seems to be to find someone who looks as though they belong in Business Class! So make like you belong!*

*As many people do when travelling, I try to dress in comfortable clothes and shoes, but I make sure that they are not 'Sloppy Joes'. Casual smart and clean is what I aim for. A light jacket and pressed trousers without creases, a shirt that has not had several days wear and that is not crumpled and clean shoes. I met a lady on one upgrade, (who had also been upgraded) she was smartly but casually dressed and looked comfortably elegant.*

*By the time you get to the counter, it is probably too late. In my case it has been the check-in supervisor who picked me. In each case this was the person who was patrolling and marshalling the queues waiting to check-in. Oh yes, by the way one possibly two small carry on items, try not to look like a badly dressed Christmas tree, so no plastic bags full of last minute purchases."*

**Graham Hart**

## Extra legroom

If you're tall and have no idea where to sit, ask for a seat with extra legroom. Be aware that if offered an emergency door seat right next to a window that the bulge of the door might encroach into your space. Seats near toilets are not great either, apart from emitting nasty smells from time to time they also become a place people queue next to.

> *"If you know the model of plane well enough, and you check-in early enough, you can know the best seats for legroom. Ask for specific seats where there are only 2 abreast instead of 3 further up the plane."*
>
> **Drew**

Approach the subject with the check-in staff by being nice and polite, ask how their day is going and always smile. The legroom seats will only be allocated to tall people, reflect on Katy's comments earlier in the chapter along with a visit to http://www.seatguru.com for some ideas of where to sit.

> *"Being tall I thought I'd done well getting a seat right at the front of the plane. I was disappointed to find out that the toilet wall was right in front of my seat and I could not stretch my legs out."*
>
> **Brian, Colchester**

## Security

Once you're returned your baggage trolley to a trolley bay and have your boarding pass ready the next challenge you face is airport security. Security points are there for all our safety and typically you will be required to walk through a metal detector while hand baggage is scanned. Security queues can be long, and before getting to the point where a check takes place you will be required to show your boarding card and passport.

> *"Security queues have a habit of levelling off at the back - as they are all equally long. But it is worth taking a moment to count the scanners at the front of the queue as usually two scanner queues go twice as fast as one*

*scanner queues, but when you join the queues they will all be the same length. One minute to look can result in 20 minutes saved."*

**Stephen Heppell**

An excellent demonstration on how the metal detector you walk through works is available at: http://tinyurl.com/3lw6ut. Clicking 'Next Page' on the site will demonstrate the bag scanning which is going on.

*"Tell the security staff that you would prefer to carry undeveloped film roles from your camera in your pocket when going through security to avoid interference from x-ray equipment. Don't forget that x-ray is used to check suitcases too, so keep all film with you in person."*

**Jo**

As you approach your turn to be checked by security please prepare yourself, there are so many annoying people who hold up queues by emptying pockets, removing coats and doing things that they could have been done while in the queue.

Approaching the front of the queue:

- remove your jacket/coat;

- turn mobile phone off and store in hand luggage; and

- remove all metal items, including belts and small change and place them in the provided tray (if male be careful not to drop your trousers if you have to remove your belt).

At the front of the queue:

- remove laptop from case if requested and place it in a tray (essential in New Zealand);

- inform security staff of any metal contained within your body from medical operations;

- don't get annoyed if you are body searched;

- if your bag is searched further request it is done so in your presence;

- answer any questions honestly and truthfully; and

- if you are allergic to dogs tell security staff before you are subject you to a sniffer dog test.

If your bags are unpacked they won't be repacked and you'll have to do this yourself, neatly packed hand luggage is easy to repack.

*"I always get stuck behind the amazing person who has, surprise surprise, not got their passport to hand in the queue for passport control. Put your passport somewhere that is easily accessible and safe and help keep the queue moving."*

**Joan**

## Terminal

Once you are through security you will generally be in the main terminal of the airport. Everyone around you either works at the airport, or is bound for a flight, in airport terminology this means you have moved from 'landside' to 'airside' in the system.

Familiarise yourself with your new surroundings, you'll be amazed what is available for you to see and do. Massages, nail bars, movies, golfing lessons, prayer rooms, and video game rooms are just some of the amenities available to outbound flyers. You'll also be mixing with transit passengers that have recently landed and are resting or on route to somewhere else.

The first rule of your new location is to expect to pay more for food, literature and travel essentials (including plug adapters and travel pillows). Find the information screens informing of the current state of outbound flights and discover if the departure gate for your flight has been allocated, it might be listed already on your boarding pass.

Unless you are late there will be some time before being called to the departure gate. With that time you could...

- Explore the airport looking for suitable places to sleep for future travellers arriving at the airport. Write up your findings at http://www.sleepinginairports.com at a later date.

- Walk to the gate (if you know it) you are departing from, time how long it takes to get there, and walk back.

- Convert all the numbers on your mobile telephone to home country friendly dialing numbers. If you plan to use your UK mobile abroad to call a UK number you'll need to swap the first zero of the telephone number for +44 (for example; '07666' would become '+44766').

- Use the telephone to call friends and family.

- Use the toilet; not all departure gates have toilets and once you are checked into the gate waiting area you won't be able to go back through easily.

- Talk to fellow travellers.

- Explore the shops and restaurants.

- Write a blog entry on an internet terminal (usually incorporated into a public telephone).

- Walk around! You will be on the plane for hours, make use of your freedom!

- Take any pre-flight medication, including travel sickness pills.

Whenever you are doing any of the above continue to stay alert to instructions for your flight on the information screens, and listen out for any announcements. On my blog I've linked through to funny airport announcements, worth a listen: http://tinyurl.com/5d9rrd.

> "Wireless internet services will be available at most international terminals, you'll need to buy a card which will give you access, and of course you'll need a laptop with wireless capability."
>
> **Kim**

Prior to flying some people will head into the bar and do their best to get drunk. Airlines will refuse to fly a passenger if they consider them over intoxicated. If you are going to have a drink to 'steady your nerves' limit yourself to 'just the one'. Don't be the person who delays the flight because he or she is having too good a time at the bar to hear the final boarding calls.

## Delays, cancellations and overbooking

Delays happen for all kinds of reasons, including late arrival of an aircraft from its previous flight, right through to strike action by ground crew and adverse weather conditions. Delays sometimes turn into flight cancellations.

Overbooking also happens from time to time, this is when too many seats are sold than actually available. The airlines will bump passengers up into the business and first class seats in order to fill the plane, but in some unfortunate situations as one of the last people to check-in, you could be without a seat for the flight home.

> *"I travel on business a lot, if my flight gets cancelled rather than join the mad rush to the airlines desk in the terminal to arrange an alternate flight I call my travel agent and see if they can help me over the phone."*
>
> ### *T. Towns*

If delayed or cancelled find out and action your rights. For European Union flyers the following news item from February 2005 introduces new rights: http://tinyurl.com/62zz46.

> *"We boarded the aircraft in the USA bound for the UK and took our seats. More passengers arrived and began seating themselves around us. We found out that the plane had been over booked and the cabin crew announced an appeal for a passenger to give up their seat, stay in a complementary hotel room, and travel the following day. A few minutes later (with no volunteer) a further announcement offered a hotel room with an upgraded seat in business class for a flight the following day, still nobody came forward. The next offer included the same as the last one, with a free return flight. Four people got up from their seats and rushed to the announcer."*
>
> ### *Dave*

To summarise for European Union member state travellers...

- Domestic or charter flights disrupted are legally entitled to cash payouts.

- If a flight is cancelled or overbooked airlines must give

out leaflets to effected passengers explaining rights and compensation allowance.

• Passengers are entitled to free food, drink and (limited) communication with others outside the airport while waiting for a delayed flight.

• If a flight is cancelled or overbooked then passengers should be offered a ticket refund, a flight home if necessary (at no charge) or payment for transport to destination.

• Passengers can request a hotel room if appropriate, and if the delay is more than five hours in length. The airline should also give a refund on the ticket, and arrange transport home.

Check the above information as regulations may have changed, and are dictated by the circumstances surrounding the delay or cancellation. If the delay or cancellation is not the fault of the airline they will not have to pay out.

By asking the airline for the fact sheet you'll be able to find out exactly what situation you are in; if no fact sheets are available ask to speak to the duty manager.

Travellers from countries outside the US will find out more at: http://tinyurl.com/4vorx3.

# Faith prayer rooms

Large airports will offer spaces for different faiths to pray; the direction of Mecca will be marked. Heathrow airport has prayer rooms in every terminal and a large number of chaplains from multiple faiths, including Jewish, Islamic, Sikh, Hindu, Catholic and Anglican. The Salvation Army also have representatives working at the airport and a counselling room and other services are also available.

The International Association of Civil Aviation Chaplains (IACAC) is a global network of Airport Chaplains. The web site provides links to worldwide airport Chaplaincies. Check out http://www.iacac.ws online.

> "I find the faith room as a haven of peace in a busy airport."

> **John**

## Duty free

You'll usually need to present your flight boarding card each time you purchase something from a duty free store. Arrival customs have limit allocations as to what you can take with you into their country.

> *"I travel so often now that I buy any compact technology or gadgets tax-free at the airport."*
>
> **George**

Buy within your means and also within your permitted allowance.

## Proceeding to gate

As soon as a departure gate number or letter is flashed up next to your flight number (on the departure information screens) passengers sharing your flight will head for the gate. The instruction on the screen next to the flight number will be something like 'Proceed to Gate' it will later convert to 'Boarding', or if you are unlucky it will read 'Delayed' or 'Cancelled' instead.

On arrival at the gate you'll be asked to present your passport and boarding card, and some airports will have compulsory or random security checks which include body and bag searches. As usual, obey all instructions and be polite at all times.

Next you'll be faced by lots of seats, of which some will be very close to the door which will lead you to the aircraft. Sit near that door if you want to be one of the first onto the aircraft. There are advantages and disadvantages for getting on board as quickly as possible, some passengers prefer to be the last on board to spend as little time as possible on the aircraft, I prefer to be first on and last off.

## Departure gate

Before boarding row numbers are announced this will be the last time you will be able to use your mobile telephone, finish up any calls, switch the phone off.

Don't leave baggage on a seat while you wander round, do not ask other passengers to watch your baggage for you. Asking other people to watch your stuff also puts those people in an uncomfortable position; your baggage is your responsibility.

Wait for your boarding call. If business class passengers are amongst you they will generally be called first, followed by passengers with children. Next the airline will call a bank of rows, listen carefully for your number. I like to be first when my row number is called so I can get onto the plane and claim my seat and store my hand luggage directly above it.

*"I like to stay in the lounge, with my laptop plugged into the mains, until the very last! I figure they will always give me a final call and once I get around the corner there is always a queue anyway so you haven't exactly delayed proceedings... I just hate queues; I want to avoid them and spend the minimum time in the plane possible!*

*Also, charging your laptop on the plane - the new Airbus A340-600 has in-flight charging facilities without having to buy one of those silly and expensive adaptors. You just plug in between the seats! The socket takes US, Australia and UK plugs (very clever) but my Apple iBook charger didn't have enough clearance to fit in. Next time I'll take my US adaptor or an extension!"*

**Dunstan, Sydney**

As your ticket is checked and split into two you'll be given the smaller stub and the aircrew will retain the bigger part of the ticket, a final passport check might also be required.

*"On route to the plane there are sometimes newspaper racks offering free titles from the flights country of origin and sometimes from its destination. These newspapers will be in limited supply so being quick on to the plane will help to get the title you want.*

*If the crew give out the papers when you are seated you'll probably get the title you want if you sit near the front of the plane, they usually run out of the good ones by the time they reach the back."*

**Julia**

As you queue for the plane in the tunnel be sure to hold the remaining part of your ticket and show it to the aircrew greeting you at the plane door as it will help them point you in the direction of your seat. Try and say hello to the airline team in their native language, they'll appreciate the effort.

## Final boarding calls

Airlines will announce by name passengers that have checked in but not arrived at the gate over the PA system. It is not uncommon that the Captain will announce to boarded passengers that the delayed takeoff is caused by a slow arriving passenger and that the passengers baggage will be offloaded if the passenger does not arrive within the next few minutes. If the late arrival baggage is offloaded that passenger will not be allowed to fly, but even worse is the look he or she will get from delayed passengers as they take their seat.

Don't be late!

## Taking your seat

When travelling alone I try to get to my seat before the passenger allocated the seat next to me arrives. By arriving first I get access to the central 'arm rest' which passengers are unsure which seat it belongs to; usually three seats in a row have four arm rests in total, one more than needed, so who gets to use it? Arriving first also means I get to put my bag directly above my seat in the overhead bin which enables easy access throughout the flight.

Always use both hands when placing and retrieving bags from the overhead bins to avoid straining yourself.

Watch out for passengers who ignore the seat allocated on their ticket and try and sit anywhere, this is often common with the passengers who are lazy or slow to get on the plane, they'll look for rows of empty seats and sit down in hope nobody claims the seat they have sat in. If you arrive at your seat and find someone in it make sure you don't sit anywhere else, as this will confuse the allocated seating even more! Ask airline staff for support if the person in your seat refuses to move.

I walked onto an plane to find a lady had sat in the seat I'd got to the airport extra early to secure. The slim tiny lady was sitting in my specially requested exit row aisle seat, with bundles of legroom. Her actual ticket showed she was due to sit in a seat four rows behind mine, next to a big well built man who she had obviously seen and decided she was not going to sit next to for fifteen hours. She suggested I took her allocated seat and pointed out that she was already comfortable. I stood my ground and said: "No, I'm tall and have specifically asked for legroom, and it is non-negotiable." I'm six foot two, she appeared to be four foot nothing.

She eventually moved causing as much fuss as possible, especially when she took her hand luggage from directly above my seat and found that there was no room for it above the seat she had been allocated. "This is really inconvenient" she said glaring at me as if I'd committed a big crime. "Have a nice flight" was my parting words as I left her complaining to the stewardess that her hand luggage had to be placed on the other side of the aeroplane. "Good on you" said the man in the neighbouring seat as I sat down, "Her perfume was overpowering, made me feel sick."

*"Don't cake yourself in perfume or aftershave please when you board a plane, other passengers sitting really close might not want to sniff your scent for ten hours, it gives me a headache when a whiff is really strong."*

**Jack, Newcastle**

How to survive a long haul flight

# 5

# Airborne

**"Flying may not be all plain sailing, but the fun of it is worth the price."**
*Amelia Earhart (1897 - 1937)*

## Takeoff

Before our status changes from 'airside' to 'airborne' we've got to do that little exciting bit in the middle known as 'takeoff'. Listen carefully to the announced safety instructions, watch the demonstrations and read the safety card which is located in the seat pocket. Look around you to identify your nearest emergency exit as it might be behind you. Ensure your seat is upright and tray table is securely stowed and the seat belt is fastened. Double check your mobile telephone is switched off.

> *"If you have a PDA which also has phone capabilities the airline will sometimes not accept that you have just disabled the telephone part of the PDA and ask you to turn the equipment off for the duration of the flight."*

> *Joey*

If you are a nervous flyer consider popping on the issued headphones, tuning into one of the radio stations, close your eyes, wait till the aircraft has reached cruising altitude and the captain has signified it is safe to unfasten seat belts. Just before take-off is the time to start sucking on a boiled sweet or begin chewing gum to help combat the potential ear popping sensation. Don't give gum to small children in case they swallow it. Babies can be made to feel more comfortable by drinking from a bottle during take off and landing; consult a doctor for baby travelling advice.

*"For me yawning removes the popping in ears during takeoff better than any other means."*

**Hamish, Italy**

If when taking off you notice some passengers sitting with their mouths open they are simply keeping the pressure the same on the inside and outside of the ears, this is their way of reducing the popping effect. Those passengers look silly, but they are really pretty smart.

*"On a recent Virgin flight I was comforted by a provided radio channel dedicated to tips, help and advice for nervous flyers like me."*

**Joey**

As the aircraft thunders along the runway there will be a lot of noise and if you are lucky enough to have a window seat towards the back of the plane you'll be able to see the wings adjusting as the aircraft lifts into the air. Once in the air you might hear the thud of the landing gear reclining into the aircraft to improve aerodynamics for the flight.

If luggage bins come open during the take off do not stand up and close them, airline staff should have spotted if a bin has swung open and will make a decision what to do. If a bin has opened directly above you raise your arm to protect your head from the dangers of potentially falling luggage.

*"Just after take-off is the when I change my watch time to the time of the destination and begin the transition into the time zone I'm flying."*

**Jenny**

Once airborne (and the captain has switched off the seat belt warning light) kick off your shoes (if your feet don't smell!), sit back and enjoy the flight. If you are suffering from ear trouble ask for advice from the aircrew on what to do.

## Sardines at altitude

When flying long haul I sometimes reflect on my immediate surroundings and feel like I'm being punished for doing something naughty...

- I've been locked inside a tube of metal behind a big door with a few of my essential worldly belongings;

- food times are dictated, served on a plastic tray;

- I eat what I'm given and there are not always second helpings;

- I've got no direct sunlight of feeling of fresh air on my face;

- I can't text or telephone home;

- I'm told by a little orange light if I'm allowed to move about, or go to the toilet;

- my exercise yard is a stretch of aisle between rows of people who I'm carefully trying not to brush against, trip over, or wake up;

- I cant always change the TV channel and therefore watch what everybody else is watching;

- lights are turned on and off at designated sleeping times; and

- I can't leave till I'm told to.

Instead of putting low risk criminals in prisons for years we could simply send them on long haul flights for at least a week solid every time they offend; we wouldn't even need to put the planes airborne!

> *"As soon as I'm on board I take off my shoes and switch to big non-slip comfy socks."*

> ***Rita***

We've heard from a booking advisor, loads of travellers and a check-in agent, how about a stewardess? Lets hear from 'Lucy'.

*"I joined the airline because I wanted to see the world. The application process was very tough, I was challenged in many ways to define how suitable I was for the demanding role. Once successful I spent weeks on courses dealing with all manners of situations from how to evacuate an aeroplane in an emergency, comfort a nervous flyer, deal with the passenger who attempts to smoke in a toilet right through to resolving seating issues with those passengers that think they can sit anywhere other than their allocated seat on a fully booked flight.*

*There are two kinds of passengers, those that are on their outbound journey and those heading home, its quite easy to spot which is which, those going home generally are more relaxed, usually exhausted and demand less attention. Those going home dream about their own bed while those on their outbound journey are usually excited at the prospect of new experiences and adventures.*

*In economy class we all feel compromised at all times. I don't think some realise how patient and how thick-skinned airline staff learn to become in order to deal with some of the abuse my colleagues and I come face to face with every day. Don't get me wrong, 99 percent of passengers are wonderful people, but I think on average one in every hundred seems to be a little more demanding. If you are unhappy with my service please don't shout at me.*

*That one person in 99 will usually forget that I too am challenged by limited space as they try to get past me while I'm holding a jug full of boiling hot water as I top up other passengers tea cups. If you're on my flight and you want to go to the toilet, that's great, just please try to hold on till after meal times.*

*During my breaks I don't have much space to retreat to, if the flight is not full I sometimes go and sit with a traveller who is on their own and have a chat, it all helps pass the time. I make a new friend, and learn some more things about other cultures. I particularly enjoyed it when an elderly lady I was chatting with left her seat to go and get me a drink, that made me smile for the rest of the flight,*

*I've met some amazing people.*

*Talking of drinks, if a fellow passenger approaches you asking if you could go and get him or her an alcoholic drink, please be cautious, we might have refused to serve that person any more alcohol because they have had too much already.*

*If you feel unwell during a flight, don't keep it to yourself, let me know, I'm more than happy to help you with any discomfort you might be in. Press the button in the panel above you to call me and I'll come over and talk with you, if you want to talk to me privately and it is safe to walk around, come and find me, I'll probably be behind one of the curtains preparing drinks.*

*I find its easier to use the button to call me than to try and stop me while I'm on another errand, I will get round to you when I'm free from my current task.*

*In the rare event of a sudden loss of cabin pressure the masks will descend from the panel above. Grab the mask, and pull it over your face. If you have a child please ensure you secure your mask before assisting with theirs.*

*We try and acclimatise you to your next time zone as best as possible, that's why we ask you to close the window blinds during daylight and we dim the lights in the cabin, try and get some sleep, you'll appreciate it.*

*I'm also amazed by the number of celebrities who fly economy, if you get a minute, have a good walk around the aeroplane (but not during mealtimes!) and see if you can spot one, but respect their privacy if you do.*

*Sit back, relax, and you'll have a great flight."*

***Lucy***

## Meat, two veg and a plastic fork

Mealtimes in the sky are not everyone's cup of tea, especially when the cup is tiny, made of plastic and balanced between a small bread roll and something that looks like a sausage. The sausage does look tasty, but I'm not sure about the strangely coloured sauce it is swimming in, which in turn is complemented by a dollop of mashed potato that looks like it was thrown from a great height in to the silver tray dish.

We've put a man on the moon, managed to clone ourselves, and can travel anywhere in the world at over thirty thousand feet... but we still can't make a meal tray dish which opens easily. I love to hate airline food, its either very good or very bad, there does not seem to be a happy medium.

> *"I am not a vegetarian but I noticed that veggie food is usually served first and is usually much better than the non-vegetarian stuff, so on planes I'm a proud token veggie!"*
>
> *Sandra*

One of the worst moments has to be when the food is served up, mealtime on a jumbo has to be the smelliest time on the plane. For at least an hour there is a lingering smell of something like beef, you'll know what I mean when you smell it for yourself, even when beef is not on the menu! The worse bit has to be when the meal is served as I'm trying to watch the in-flight film. Complicating it even more is when passengers decide to go and relieve themselves in the middle of the meal serving time, trying to squeeze past the food trolley.

Worst still is when I'm sitting in the middle of three seats and I'm challenged to eat my airline meal without moving my elbows in case I invade the space of my neighbours, who I've hardly spoken to, and are probably still trying to work out exactly which of the arm rests is theirs.

> *"One good thing about food time in flight is that the overpowering smell of passengers collective meals cover the overpowering perfume smell from the lady sitting in front who has absolutely no consideration for those around her as she pumps way too much of her smelly scent into the air!"*
>
> *Grumpy Gramps*

# Travel sickness and turbulence

Sometimes the Captain will be aware of possible turbulence in advance, and other times turbulence will be unexpected. At 35,000 feet turbulence is pretty rare, you're more likely to suffer from it on a smaller plane on a short flight.

*"During turbulence sit upright, relax your shoulders and sip a water bottle."*

**Karen**

Fortunately for me I don't get travel sick. As kids my family would often drive over 200 miles down to Weymouth in Dorset on the Southern coast of the UK, we would spend the summer there. On one particular journey when both my younger brother and I were really small we both felt really ill during the bumpy and windy roads. As mum stopped the car at a railway crossing we both promptly threw up at the same time into the cupped hands of our alert Dad, we were about six and four years old. Dad said he'll never forget that moment and frequently recalls it. At the time of the incident we were less than one mile from our destination accommodation.

*"I once felt really sick and reached for the sick bag I expected to be in the seat pocket in front of me, and it was not there. Luckily the person sitting next to me gave me theirs. I now always check to make sure the sick bag is in place before take off!"*

**Stella**

Flying on a connecting flight between Queenstown and Christchurch in New Zealand I experienced my first ever plane journey which was turbulent for the majority of the flight. The plane was very small and had propellers mounted on the wings, it was the first flight I'd ever been on that I generally felt sick. The man in the seat next to me was also feeling unwell, claiming to never in his life experienced travel sickness. He told me that he'd been drinking excessively the previous night and really regretted it now. Due to the aeroplane being in unusually bad turbulence the pilot announced that for the safety of his crew no food or drink service would be operating for the duration of the journey.

I think the only reason myself and the stranger in the seat next to me survived that turbulent flight without throwing up was due to me having a couple of bottles of water in my hand luggage. I gave one of the bottles to my new friend who continually thanked me each time he sipped it. The water helped sooth the horrible dry sickness taste in my mouth. Ever since that flight I've had my bottle of water to hand, when it is half full I ask the airline crew to refill it, or I go and refill it myself, stretching my legs at the same time.

> *"I find seats over the wings are far more comfortable during turbulence."*
>
> **Mahesh**

On the same flight I had the utmost respect for the aircrew member who left her seat to provide a continuous supply of sick bags to a Japanese lady. I don't personally think I'd be able to say 'thank you' each time somebody handed me a bag of sick, but she did and her customer service from the moment we boarded to the moment we departed the aircraft was the best in-flight service I'd ever experienced from a lone crew member anywhere in the world; Air New Zealand have always employed the very best in my opinion.

> *"In a past life I was a teacher. One effective tip we used with children feeling travel sick on school trips was to bring the unwell child to the front of the coach, we would ask him or her to sit on a newspaper. If your children are feeling unwell, give it a try."*
>
> **Hal**

Consider the following if you are feeling travel sick...

- Tell a crew member! If the plane suffers from turbulence a good crew will come and see how you are as soon as the bumpy patch has passed.

- Carry a bottle of water with you and keep it topped up each time it gets to being only half full, never let a water bottle be empty when turbulence hits.

- Store your water bottle in the seat pocket in front of you, if the aircraft hits turbulence as soon as its taken off you won't be allowed to undo that seat belt and rummage around in the overhead bin looking for that vital bottle.

- Avoid alcohol and stay well hydrated with water.

- During turbulence you'll be instructed to move your seat back into the upright position, sit up, lean back, close your eyes.

- Distract yourself through listening to music or holding conversation with fellow passengers.

- If you've not asked for a seat over the wings, and notice one is available, ask if you can move to it, the journey will be less bumpy.

- Travel sickness tablets will be available at most chemists, check with your doctor if you are unsure about taking them, especially if you plan to take tablets which will help you to sleep.

*"Flying over India I experienced turbulence for the very first time as we fell what felt like miles out of the sky, my stomach leapt and turned and tried to escape. I went into autopilot, grab sick bag, grab sick bag, where is the sick bag? Grab anything, grab handy blanket for keeping legs warm!*

*As I tried to hand my sick parcel to the stewardess she smiled, 'Could you take this please? I'm afraid I've been sick and I couldn't find a sick bag.' Her smile continued unbroken and still the blanket remained in my possession. It was becoming clear that her English wasn't great and my attempt at her native language was rubbish. The only language that could unite us now was the international language of charades. I started. My sick act was good and she got it straight away, however my toothbrush needed work.*

*The stewardess left only to return minutes later with a male colleague. Once again I acted out the brushing my teeth, he got it straight away, he'd obviously played this game before."*

**James Taylor, Norwich**

## Sleeping

To sleep easily you'll firstly need to feel as comfortable as possible and second actually tired. When you head to bed at night you spend some time making yourself comfortable, do exactly the same when you settle down to sleep on an aeroplane, but if you usually sleep nude don't do that during a flight.

> *"Do whatever you know tires you out. I personally get tired when reading in low light or undertaking difficult games of sudoku or word-searches."*
>
> **Justina**

On most international flights alcohol is free, some passengers will make the most of this service as a way of getting themselves off to sleep. The effects of alcohol at altitude is far more powerful than when you're on the ground, drink sensibly.

If you are feeling restless take a wander from your seat and go and observe how passengers seated near the emergency doors are coping and decide if you could be comfortable sitting in those seats on your return journey, Leonie explains why...

> *"Having arrived at the airport early for once, I managed to persuade the booking clerk to give me a seat next to the emergency door. Although at first it seems there isn't much leg room cos the door bulges outwards (this might not be on all flights of course) I discovered it is perfect for resting my legs on. Its a rare event for me to sleep on a long flight - but this time - I had a great sleep, stretched out with my legs kept in place by propping them against the little TV screen that usually folds under the seat.*
>
> *Another time I had a good sleep on a flight (learned from long haul train journeys in Australia as a youth), was when I flew to China. There was an empty seat between myself and a elderly Chinese woman, who was next to the window. Using sign language I negotiated that I would sleep stretched out in the foot well, while she stretched out on the seats. We both slept like logs. Mind you, you have to be careful not to trip people up with stray feet in the walk way."*
>
> **Leonie, Australia**

Lets find out how some of our other fellow passengers nod themselves off to sleep...

*"Me and the wife swap seats when we want to go to sleep, that way it helps us reposition ourselves somewhere new and get comfortable. One seat is for when we are awake, the other is for when we are asleep, vice versa for the other person, it's a bit strange, but it works for us."*

**Joe, Warwickshire**

*"Engage in conversation with any stranger to your left or right who could disturb your sleep and conclude your conversation with 'I'm going to get some sleep now', to which they might say: 'I'll just squeeze past you and stretch my legs and pop to the loo, then so I won't be interrupting you later'."*

**Laura, Auckland, NZ**

*"I always have a nice cup of tea before bed time at home, so I do the same on aeroplanes, I take my own brand of tea bag and ask for a cup of hot water and experience a familiar taste. I find trying to keep to my routine tells my body it is time for sleep."*

**Brenda**

*"Keep an eye out for rows of vacant seats and asking the crew if you can sleep on those seats there for a while."*

**Darren, Brent Cross**

*"I bring ear-plugs and an eye-mask for sleeping."*

**Anon**

*"Kick off your shoes, tune into the classical radio station, turn down the volume, shut your eyes, count sheep."*

**Marion, Newton Abbott**

*"Long Haul flights can be a nightmare and I always get cold but have found a product called the 'Cabin Cuddler'. Its a specially designed fleece blanket with a foot pocket much better than the blankets they give you on planes cos it keeps you warm all over ... a bit like a sleeping bag, but not as bulky!"*

**Alyson**

*"Make sure your belongings are safe before you go to sleep, someone stole my iPod while I was counting sheep."*

**Barry**

Seek personal medical advice if you decide to action the following tip:

*"On the plane, take calming/sleeping tables and a little wine when you should be asleep in the destination time zone, and decongestant (containing pseudoephedrine) when you should be awake. I reckon this reduces the jet lag recovery time by heaps."*

**Chris**

The passengers sitting next to me on the flight from Malaysia knocked themselves out for 7 hours using 'Night Nurse'; seek advice from a Chemist or Doctor before doing the same.

## Mealtimes

It is the moment I dislike the most, but have to bring it up again!

One person I fly with refuses point blank to eat airline food, although they will eat the chocolate desert, and mine come to think of it.

Good airlines (especially the Asian ones) will bring round hot towels for you to clean yourself prior to your meal. Being careful not to scald myself I put the towel over my face and breathe through it, this sorts out my nose, mouth and ears which have become congested by the cabin pressure air. Once I've cleared out my head, then I use the towel to clean as much of my neck and arms as I can.

*"I prefer to sit at the back of the plane and get served last at meals. I've found that passengers near the front of the plane have usually long finished their meals by the time I've been served mine. I might not get my first meal choice but I'm not that much of a fussy eater and my finished tray is in front of me for much less time as it is cleared away along with everyone else's."*

**Darren, Milton Keynes**

*"Watch this Youtube video if you want to see an example of how airline food is made: http://tinyurl.com/6kwrwy."*

**James**

*"If you sit near the front of the plane you'll be more likely to get the meal of your choice, rather than the unpopular dish after everyone else has made their selection. If the meal trolley has run out of the dish you would prefer ask the aircrew member if they could kindly check with another trolley to see if they have your choice.."*

**Anon**

# Jet lag reduction

To help with your conquest to beat jet lag you've hopefully already switched your watch to the same time at your final destination, some passengers will not do this and in my experience suffer from jet lag longer.

I try hard to eat meals in accordance with the mealtime at the final destination, preparing my body for the change. Things get a bit complicated if I'm flying to the other side of the world and a transit stop is involved, this adds a third time zone to the mix! The airline will always try and feed me at a time I don't want feeding.

I eat very little at some of the mealtimes knowing that there is usually a stash of sandwiches available somewhere on the plane if I really want to eat in accordance with my destination country.

Another jet lag essential is to try and sleep with the patterns of the destination time zone. Those that are aboard an aeroplane which is travelling towards the sun (rather than away from it) will get much more daylight compared with those flying away, who get a longer night. This is why I prefer to fly from London away from the sun (the Asia route) when going to the other side of the world.

Preparation is the best way to combat jet lag and hopefully you took into account the advice in chapter two.

# Health

> *"Seems as though I've been flying long haul for years and it gets worse all the time - but then I guess 40 years ago the seats really were more spacious. In recent years, the best flight without breaking the bank was London to Brunei, on Royal Brunei Airlines. Brilliant service, and alcohol free which helps resist the temptation to drink myself into oblivion."*

> ### *Shirley*

Good point Shirley, the effect of alcohol in the air is much more than when consumed on the ground. Both alcohol and caffeine intake will tend to dehydrate the body, so drink plenty of water. Good advice is to drink at least a bottle of water every hour, which prompts the body to walk to the toilet, an opportunity to stretch and exercise legs on route.

> *"Use a flannel and small towel to 'wash down' whilst balancing on tippy-toes in the loo. If nothing else it will make everyone sitting close by outside wonder what is going on!"*

> ### *Deborah*

Good things to do include...

- Drinking from a plastic bottle, ask the aircrew to fill it up for you when it is empty, it is much easier than drinking (and spilling) from a plastic cup supplied by the airline.

- Maintaining good circulation by avoiding sitting with legs crossed.

- Hydrating the skin by applying a moisturising lotion to hands and face.

- Standing up and walking around.

- Seat exercises.

> *"Those small cans of soda are too small, but I guess they mean less trips to the restroom."*
>
> **Mitch, USA**

## Exercise

There are lots of exercises you can do while in the air. Some airlines will show seat exercise videos which passengers are encouraged to take part in.

Example exercises to do include...

- Reach up towards the light above with your right hand, then with your left hand, repeat.

- Sit with your straight and shoulders back, put toes flat against the floor and heels slightly raised, lower one heel, followed by the other, repeat.

- Sit with your back straight in the seat and raise and lower shoulders.

- Rotate shoulders in circles.

- Cross left leg over right, rotate the elevated foot in circular motions, reverse the directions, repeat with other leg.

- Hold arms at the elbows, turn left and right, repeat.

- Explore more ideas at the following web site: http://tinyurl. com/57pab4.

Wander up and down the plane as much as you can, use the need for a regular intake of water as a good excuse to do this. Aircrews often have a supply of sandwiches and drinks available for those of us who like to snack between meals.

## Entertainment

Ideas to keep boredom at bay, stimulate the mind, and tire you out:

- exercise frequently;

- plan a road trip;

- read a book about the final destination;

- write letters to friends and family;

- plan a novel;

- wander up and down the aircraft;

- make a list of as many fruit and vegetables you can think of;

- think of a boys and girls name for every letter of the alphabet;

- play eye-spy;

- listen to soothing music;

- do a small jigsaw puzzle on the seat tray;

- write that list of things you want to do in your lifetime;

- sudoku, word searches, crosswords;

- play solitaire;

- talk to your neighbours;

- write a poem;

- make a list of people to buy gifts for;

- design a board game;

- draw;

- read the free newspaper you picked up as you boarded;

- swap the free newspaper with another passengers alternative title;

- listen to music;

- fill out your landing card; and

- write a short story about the kindest thing a stranger has ever done for you.

> *"I once had a great chat with an elderly lady who was flying from Canada to visit her son, she was travelling alone and appreciated someone to talk to and show pictures of grandchildren. She also had sweets. "*
>
> **Andrew**

I've had some great conversations in the queue for the toilet with people from Bangladesh, China and India all keen to practice their English speaking. If you are also looking for an icebreaker to talk to the stranger sitting next to you go and get a drink and ask your neighbour if they would like one too.

> *"Keep your passport to hand during the flight, you'll need it when filling out the landing forms."*
>
> **May**

# Landing cards

The United Kingdom Home Office states the following on their web site at the time of publication of this book:

> *"We will ask you to complete a landing card, unless: You are a national of the European Economic Area (EEA); or the UK is not your final destination and you do not need to go through passport control to continue your journey."*
>
> ***http://tinyurl.com/3w8x4a***

You will be asked to complete a landing card while on board the flight, it should have been provided for you by the cabin crew. Check that your completed card is correct, legible and well presented before leaving the plane.

Transit passengers are not usually required to complete landing cards for the first part of their journey, as they only stop in the transit country for a few hours and are restricted to staying in the airport.

## Landing

Buckle up, sit back, and relax as the aircraft comes in to land. Emergency landings are very rare but for maximum safety make sure you are aware of the emergency procedure listed on the safety card.

*"Sucking on a mint or chewing gum can help prevent ear popping sensations during landing. My wife bought from the chemists a device to put in her ears that helps prevent the pain caused by a change in cabin pressure."*

**Danny**

Once the aircraft has landed and begins its taxi to the arrivals terminal stay seated until the captain switches off the seat belt sign.

If you are a smoker you will not be allowed to light up until you are inside the designated smoking areas within the airport, some airports have a total ban on smoking.

*"If you have Italians on board, join in with their clapping when the plane lands, good fun!"*

**Ian**

# 6

# Transit, Arrival and Onwards

**"A good traveller has no fixed plans, and is not intent on arriving."**
*Lao Tzu, Philosopher of Ancient China*

## Land ahoy

Once you've landed for the first time you'll be challenged next with either:

- a transit stop followed by another long or short haul flight;

- leaving the international airport terminal to catch a flight from the domestic flights terminal; or

- leaving the airport as this is the final flight destination.

Lets start with transit…

## Transit

Depending on the direction around the world flown, and how long the total journey is, it might not be possible to get to a final destination in just one long haul flight, a transit stop is necessary.

If on a split flight journey you will find yourself landing roughly half way, your status will now change to being a 'transit passenger'.

Along with other transit passengers on your flight you will have to disembark with all your personal belongings and navigate the transit airport to find the next flight for your journey.

When you leave the plane follow the signs for 'Transit Passengers', or 'Flight Connections', else you will find yourself heading into passport control, immigration and customs. Ask staff for support if you are unsure where to go. While in transit you are subject to the host country laws.

Before I experienced long haul for myself I thought that the luxury of a shower while in transit airports was exclusive to those travelling in business and first class. If only I'd known that some of the services in the airport offer a private lounge, internet access, shower and snack food to economy passengers for a relatively small charge. After a refreshing shower, bite to eat, free drinks and a quick check of the email I was able to go to shut my eyes for a while. When it was time for me to leave I was woken by the friendly staff on hand to make my stay with them as pleasant as possible, all part of the service.

> *"I had an eight dollar shower in Singapore which was fantastic, definitely recommend that!"*
>
> **Tom Smith, Yorkshire**

Of course duty free, local culture shops, massages, food outlets and communication services are also available for the weary traveller to spend their time in transit, all helping the local economy. Changi Airport in Singapore even boasts a swimming pool for passengers to enjoy between flights!

> *"The airport itself was horrible, but then again I hadn't slept in about twenty four hours. Looking back now I think it was the closest I've ever been to going insane. My body wanted to shut down my brain had already signed off. I had another eight hours to sit and wait, I seem to remember counting the tiny lizards climbing the walls. The seats in the airport were cruel, plastic with little backing and hard metal arm rests. I would have got on a plane back to England if there was one going, I was getting pretty desperate. For some much needed energy I searched for food after exchanging a small amount of Australian dollars for a million of the local currency.*

*In my sleepless stupor I managed to get my hands on some highly nutritious 'Pringles' and 'Oreos', I think I was attracted to the different packaging rather than the contents. However, the mixture of salt, sugar and chemicals perked me up, I felt a little bit lighter and brighter, I could focus my eyesight and fix my gaze on the departure screen. Only another six hours to wait."*

**James Taylor, Norwich**

I watched the most amazing sunset in Kuala Lumpar airport while waiting at the gate for the final leg of my journey. The airport also has a rainforest in the middle which environmentalist David Bellamy (who sat in the seat behind me on the outbound flight) took great delight in showing me.

*"If you are a smoker this one goes a long way.... If someone is stopping for re-fuel in Singapore, not a lot of people know that there is a 'tropical oasis' in an outdoor area of the transit terminal ....it also has a bar!!! It's a great place even if you don't smoke as it sprays light mist on you for the mossies and you get to chat to a lot of travellers!"*

**Donna**

*"After the recent terrorist threats associated to the United States expect higher levels of security at US airports whether you are arriving, in transit, or departing."*

**Ben**

If the United States of America is playing host as your transit airport the chances are you will be required to collect your hold baggage from a baggage carousel and travel with it while officials scan it, you might be questioned on the contents of your luggage. Once officials are satisfied that your luggage poses no threat you will then be required to pass it back to the care of the airline where it will be put in the hold of your next aircraft.

*"My four year old gets very restless when we travel to see her Nan in the USA. I bought her a hand luggage bag with built in seat which she tows along and sits on when we are in long queues or waiting in transit, she loves it!"*

**Kat**

## Transit hotels

Hotel accommodation at large airports is usually available in the transit airport too, so you'll have the opportunity to lay flat for a few hours and get some sleep if the gap between your flights is long enough. You will need to book your hotel room in advance if you want to guarantee availability.

> *"Transit hotel rooms can be quite expensive as these hoteliers appreciate that when we're really tired we'll pay a premium."*

> **Chris**

## Culture sightseeing

Short sightseeing tours are also available from some transit airports, Singapore Changi Airport offers excellent sightseeing tours. If the wait between flights is more than four hours transit passengers have the opportunity to take part in a colonial tour or a cultural tour, both tours are free. The airport also boasts exotic performances and events and really is a great place to stop.

## Reboarding

You will have listened carefully to any announcement and be promptly waiting at the correct gate where you might be searched, scanned and have your passport and boarding card checked before boarding the aircraft for the next leg of your journey. You won't always be sitting in the same seat as your last flight, and will be offered either breakfast, lunch, or dinner (after take off) depending on the local time of departure, this will help confuse your body clock even more!

> *"When arriving at the airport for a flight from London to Australia the check-in agent allocated me the same seat for the first flight to Singapore as the second flight to Sydney."*

> **James**

## Domestic connecting flights

If you are due to catch a connecting flight to take you to a destination in the same country you will probably need to leave the international airport terminal and enter the domestic flights terminal. For this process you will navigate passport control, collect baggage and then go through customs.

If you checked baggage to the final destination you won't necessarily see it here unless the landing airport requires the baggage to be re-checked. Ask for advice from airport ground staff on where you should go and what you should do to catch your connecting flight.

Your connecting flight won't necessarily be with the same airline you flew half way around the world with. A little later we'll hear from Jonathan, a British passenger who missed his connecting flight while he was probed by customs.

> *"One thing I noticed about one European domestic flight airline is that in the very back row of their planes the seats don't recline, and you are also not allowed any bags or coats to be stowed by your feet. Unless you plan on having a really good conversation with the other people in your row try to avoid that particular part of the plane. Then again, when you land you might be disembarked through the rear doors of the plane - and the back row aisle seats are a prime location to get off first!"*
>
> ### *McCarthorse Cattleclub*

> *"American Airlines provide headphones for free on International flights, but on internal USA flights they charge around $5 a pair, keep where possible the international flight headphones and use them on the internal connecting flights."*
>
> ### *Julie, Rochester*

## Passport control

Between the landing gate and the queues of weary looking people all waiting to have their passports stamped are usually some toilets, you might want to relieve yourself before heading into what can be a long and pretty intensive process.

You will be directed by signs in two directions, something like 'Citizens' and 'International Visitors'. Obviously the queue you join will be 'International Visitors', unless of course you hold a valid local passport for this country. Once in the queue ensure you have any completed paperwork ready in your hand along with your passport. Check the paperwork you have is neat and legible, remember you are looking to impress your host country.

Family members who live in the same household are often able to meet with passport control as a group, which saves some time as all applications to be dealt with at the same time, this process differs dependent on the host country procedure. The United States has a 'no waiting' policy in place, which means you are not allowed to wait for other passengers who are being processed once your application has been completed, you'll have to walk through to the baggage hall and wait for them there.

Once you are at the front of the queue wait to be called by the representative, approach and exchange pleasantries, do not lean on or across the counter. Answer all questions professionally, co-operate if your fingerprint and pupil scans are requested. In a situation where your application is questionable by your potential host country you can expect to be guided to a waiting area where officials will question you further. Co-operate as best to your ability, ask what support is available if you feel misunderstood.

*"Suck on a breath mint before meeting the passport control representative, I would hate to be that poor person trying to do their job while an aircraft full of people who have not brushed their teeth for hours come rolling past!"*

**Ben**

# Baggage collection

I absolutely hate this bit, especially in busy international airports.

Crowds of weary eyed tired and irritated passengers scramble around the baggage carrousels with their eyes focused on the point where the bags appear from and then drop down onto the moving belt.

Before even finding a place to squeeze between other people to eagerly watch for a bag arriving you'll have to find the right belt first, look up at the screens and follow the directions.

If lots of flights are landing at the airport around the same time the belt will often already be rotating (usually with obscure items still unclaimed from the previous flight). I always feel very sorry for the owners of the big battered red box, long green tube, or bright orange rucksack whose stuff has arrived either in the wrong country, or the owner is still trying to get through passport control to claim it.

Once the first item of luggage is ready to show its head a siren will alarm and the belt will scream into life. I love this bit, now you can watch all the other passengers opposite you and to the left and right shuffle forward as if they expect their bag to appear first, ready and waiting with their arms free to grab it. Once the baggage starts appearing enjoy the moment watching lots of travellers who all brought almost identical looking black suitcases pointing out what they think belongs to them, moving along the belt towards them, they grab it, check the tag, shake their head and then let it go on its way down the belt before grabbing exactly the same case and check it again each time it comes past.

> *"At the airport I spotted what looked like my black suitcase on the belt coming towards me. Just before it got to me another man picked it off the luggage belt and started to walk off with it. I ran after him and said... 'that is my case' to which he said... 'no it's not, it is mine!' so we checked the label and he said 'sorry' and walked back to the belt, I dread to think what would have happened if I'd not spotted him get to my case first.*
>
> *I can't believe that someone would be silly enough to assume they were the only person to have a black case made by a well known luggage manufacturer, and therefore not need to check the tags. I mark my suitcase now with colourful shoelaces tied to the handle."*
>
> ### Sarah

Although your luggage was checked in at the same time as a friend or family member don't expect it to arrive in a neat little line on the belt, the ground crew that loaded the aircraft will have packed the luggage into the hold in a way that will maximise the use of the space available, and because of this bags and cases will come out in no particular order.

The first items on the belt are usually the priority baggage items, such as child seats, buggies and pushchairs for children. If you loaded a fragile item onto the aircraft check with airport staff where to collect the item.

'Business' and 'First Class' passengers will not have to wait long for their bags, usually waiting somewhere separate from the economy passengers for their luggage to be brought out to them.

## Missing baggage

Not all baggage will arrive, some baggage will be lost, hopefully not forever. A little known fact is that some baggage will arrive in advance of you, for example if you have flown on a flight with a transit stopover but your luggage has flown on another flight which is direct to your final destination, don't ask why airlines do it, but sometimes this happens. I once turned up really early at Stansted airport for a short flight to Geneva in Switzerland, I checked in really early and my bag left on the flight before mine, without me knowing.

After waiting at the Geneva carousel for ages, and spending time queued up with other worried passengers looking for their stuff I eventually spoke with an airline representative, and logged my details. While this was happening a colleague of mine had took the initiative to search the other carousels and trolleys loaded up around the baggage room, these trolleys were filled with stray cases, mine was amongst them. What concerned me was that my case would have arrived on the earlier flight and probably spent time travelling around the carousel before eventually being taken off and loaded on to a trolley.

> *"If your bag is missing you will need to talk with a baggage claims representative as soon as possible, ask the person you speak with to trace your luggage."*
>
> **Phil**

Http://www.thetravelinsider.info offers sound advice when it comes to delays and lost baggage, go to the web site and type the following into the search box:

• 'Your rights if your bags are delayed'

• 'Your rights if your bags are lost by the airlines'

The site offers a 'suggested claim strategy', one of the key lessons it shares is the need to provide as much information as possible for the airline to locate and make contact with you.

While working in Asia I got a call from Justina who had just arrived in North America, her bright pink suitcase had not arrived. American Airlines told her that her suitcase had been located and was travelling on the following flight and that once it had arrived at the airport it would be delivered to her hotel at no charge. The suitcase arrived at her hotel the very next day. Advice here is simple; pack some of your clothing in the cases of other people you are travelling with, if your case is delayed you will still have clothing you can wear.

> *"I take a photograph of my luggage with me. If it gets lost I can attach the photograph to the lost luggage form and help the airline identify it quicker."*
>
> **Richard S**

> *"In a situation where you are travelling alone and your case has not arrived at your destination ask the airline what they will do to compensate you for the inconvenience of not having clean clothing and toiletries."*
>
> **Ben**

Over 350 world airlines and their handling agents use the 'World Tracer' system, a global database of lost bags. If you search around the internet some airlines will redirect you to their portal within the system and allow customers to input their 'File Reference' and 'Name' into a web page for lost luggage, this will find the latest information held about specified bags, if information exists.

> *"My suitcase did not turn up on the conveyer belt, and after twenty minutes of watching the same unclaimed orange bag and a dirty old trainer going round and round on the belt I began enquiring as to where it might be. I was pointed in the direction of the 'Oversized and Unusual Baggage Claim Desk'. It turns out that my suitcase had split open, I could see it on the rack shelving behind the desk, in a clear plastic sack."*
>
> **Lucas**

## Damaged baggage

When reunited with your luggage check for any damage or signs of tampering. If the bag is damaged take it to the airline representative immediately and ask them to record your concern and provide you with information on what happens next. The airline might decide to replace the damaged item via a luggage repair company, you will be required to keep the receipt when invoicing the airline for the repair if payment is made by you, keep a copy of the receipt.

The airline might choose to replace the damaged item and provide you with a choice of alternative new items from which to pick, ask what guarantee comes with the replacement item.

## Arrival tax

Prior to your trip through customs you may be required to queue up and pay a tax to leave the airport. Have the right money prepared. If you don't have the right money don't always expect change.

## Customs

We've learnt that the experiences of others has helped us on our travels, so lets find out the troubles we can face if we don't do the simple things that help customs staff do their job.

Jonathan Furness is a Primary School Teacher, I worked with Jonathan on a Tsunami recovery related film project in Phuket for the British Council in 2005.

After the project had completed we flew together to Bangkok and I worked there, Jonathan boarded another aeroplane to New Zealand where he would conduct some more research based work. Here is how Jonathan coped as he entered a foreign land after a two-week detour through South East Asia:

> *"With much excitement, I headed quickly towards New Zealand's immigration desks at Auckland International airport. The plane from Bangkok, via Sydney, had landed late and this left me with very little time to catch my domestic connecting flight to Christchurch.*
>
> *On arrival at immigration, passport and landing card in hand, I made the mistake of being rather too jolly with the*

*immigration official whom I recognised from my trip to NZ last year. The official, lets call him Kevin, managed to break a smile, quite unusually for an immigration official. Kevin seemed interested in my lack of documentation for my three-week stay in the country as he didn't seem satisfied with my honesty about my purpose for the visit. Visiting a friend in Christchurch without knowing the friend's home address and saying you will be "collected" from Christchurch airport wasn't a convincing story for entering a secure and safe country such as New Zealand.*

*I think there's a lesson to learn here, never enter a country without tickets or some documentation which indicates how long you intend to stay in the host country - something I was clearly lacking.*

*Kevin duly stamped my immigration card and I set off, next stop Customs... Still excited, and smiling lots I handed my landing card to the customs official, slightly perturbed and intimidated by the sheer number of security personnel and dogs who gave a very obvious presence to those who had just landed.*

*I was directed to follow a lane which appeared to be quite different to the one most others were following. It dawned on me, only a few moments later, that I was heading straight towards a large private room where I was asked to take a seat, joining a queue of other passengers, all of which looked distinctly dodgier than me.*

*Feeling anxious, intimidated, and scared I sat and trembled wondering how I'd found myself sitting in a queue for being interrogated. Unfamiliar with the customs process, I found myself asking questions to myself, did the officials find something that I wasn't aware of? Had I been framed? Had the dogs detected something? Were there items in my large holdall that I was carrying, unknowingly?*

*After about 20 minutes of nervously biting at my fingers, watching those before me emptying their bags, customs officials studying the contents to the nth degree. A few passengers had disappeared to rooms adjacent to the larger room. It had one-way windows, my imagination ran wild as I could only presume these rooms were for more intimate searches. It was then that I wanted to be anywhere but here, and it was then when I first started thinking about my escape.*

*A beckoning hand brought me to my trembling feet and I moved across the room with nervous energy.*

*I was asked not to touch the bags as the official first asked me to declare if I was carrying any items that shouldn't be. Several attempts were made to further intimidate, on the third time, I was asked to sign a piece of paper where I would commit my declaration to paper. I must have looked guiltier than a burglar caught with his hands in the till.*

*After what seemed like eternity wondering when it was my turn to endure a physical search, I was asked to sign another piece of paper and repack my luggage. The search revealed nothing, no surprise there then, and 50 minutes later, I had missed my connecting flight to Christchurch.*

*Although getting myself on the next available flight wasn't difficult, the check-in the staff were brilliant at understanding my position and putting me on the next flight. As it happened, I was on a direct flight to Christchurch unlike the booked one, which would have taken me via Wellington.*

*The message is simple. Before setting off on any international trip, ensure you have the documentation with you which ensures it details the reason for your trip, the places where you are staying, and indicates what time you will be leaving the country. You should also be more wary of travelling from countries certain countries like Thailand, as your entrance to any international country will be more closely scrutinised.*

*Always be honest, be clear and direct with airport staff. After my experience, and despite finding nothing, it is clear to me if you try to hide something you shouldn't be carrying, you will be found out.*

*Good luck and happy travelling."*

**Jonathan Furness**

Once you've collected your baggage from the belt and started heading for the exit in the baggage hall you'll head through the exit for international visitors via 'nothing to declare' or the 'declare' lane. In your home country (on your return journey) you'll need to decide if what you are carrying needs to be declared to customs, or not. If in doubt, ask a member of airport staff.

Bringing food into a country can also require declaration. When I arrived in New Zealand once I had to queue up in the 'red lane' as on my person I had a packet of sweets, which is considered 'food'. Had I not had the sweets I would have been able to travel straight through the much quieter 'green lane'. Bringing fruit and meat into New Zealand commands an instant fine.

> *"Read the advice sheet that accompanies your ticket - so far I've found 'Thomas Cook', 'First Choice', 'Virgin' Atlantic, and 'British Airways' provide the most useful information on packing and getting through the airport."*
>
> ### *Jemma*

## Freedom and onwards

As you head off on your adventure lets finish on some general travel tips to help you on your way...

- To avoid spoiling the first few days of the trip with bizarre sleeping patterns ensure you blend in with the local time zone as quickly as possible, ignore you body clock and take notice of the advice http://www.bodyclock.com suggested.

- When agreeing a price for goods or a service always ask for a price that includes tax.

- Ensure all passport and documentation are safe at all times.

- Keep your money always out of sight and don't count it in public view.

- When heading out of some airports be conscious that native traders will begin their sales pitches to generate revenue from new arrivals unfamiliar with the local economy and the cost of things, including a taxi.

- Ask at an information point within the airport building how much local taxi routes cost, taxi journeys are usually more expensive than buses.

- It is illegal in some countries to run out of fuel so keep topping up as filling stations can be long distances apart.

- Don't drive tired.

- When driving a hire car be aware that there might be toll roads on your route, have cash ready for these.

- In tourist shops in countries you might be offered free refreshments on arrival, if you don't plan to spend in the shop politely decline.

- Be prepared to say 'no thank you' to persistent sales people.

- Cook all foods at the correct temperatures, don't eat anything that looks under cooked.

- Drink bottled water rather than mains water where advised.

- Ask for 'no ice' in drinks if you are unsure of its origin (bottled or mains water).

- When using an internet café; if it is the cheapest it is probably the slowest.

- When travelling in a group to a new place (like a museum, theme park, mall, market or similar) always agree a meeting point in case somebody gets lost.

- On your last day of a package holiday it is sometimes possible to get an extended checkout on a hotel room if the airport transfer time is late in the day; this will usually cost additional money, but might not be possible if the next arrival needs the room, good hotels will offer a baggage storage room.

- When travelling on or returning home ensure suitcase tags reflect your next destination.

- Be ready to pay a departure tax at some airports, have the right cash ready, and as always, don't expect change.

- If you've been away a long time to an isolated region, you might want to check-in with your doctor on your return for a quick health check.

And finally, and most importantly:

- stay safe;

- keep on top of your finances and budget at all times; and

- have fun.

*"We studied the 'Lonely Planet' guidebook before we arrived in Lima (Peru), and were aware of the type of environment that we would be coming into. It was late evening and we arrived around 11pm. Our challenge was getting a cab to the 'trendy' Miraflores area of Lima. As we headed toward the exit door, we were inundated with cab drivers, and I mean inundated!*

*If you have seen the film 'My Big Fat Greek Wedding' then it felt like were being swarmed by a family of cab drivers, all vying for our attentions; something that we were all not used to... All we kept hearing was 'We do you good price... we are very safe!' ...At one point, we were being chased by a load of them... probably looked like a bunch of idiots running with 100 litre backpacks on our back.*

*We got to the end of the car park, realising that there was nowhere else for us to go, and then we just simply turned around and came running back toward the cab drivers!!! We found refuge within the airport, trying to devise a plan of escaping the mad rush of people vying for our money. As we looked toward the exit, there were tens of cab drivers just waving at us.*

*Our decision to try a different exit proved no better, since the same cab drivers had moved to the other exit, waving once again. In the end, we just simply ran out into the crowd of people and asked who could do us the cheapest deal... (The standard cab price was supposed to be 40 Peruvian Soles) ...and one cab driver said "$4 dollars each." Impressed, and since no one else could beat his price, we went with him.*

*The journey to the hostel was about 30 minutes and when we got there, the cabbie said $18, since he conveniently forgot to tell us that he hadn't added tax onto our price. We gave him the money and only realised after he had* *left us that we had been conned. $18 dollars in Peruvian money was about 62 Soles (even though a standard cab was supposed to be 40 soles). But hey, we were tired after a very long flight, and that cabbie was a crafty feller!"*

**Richard Pont**

# Goodbye

In my experience when it comes to long haul flights there are three classifications of passenger, and I've been all three at some point.

The first type of passenger is what I call the 'snorer', they are someone who is able to settle down, get comfortable, and sleep as and when they want to, often for most of the journey.

Next comes the 'worker', the person who sets to use their time in the air for as much productivity as possible, reading, writing, tapping away at a computer and doing all those things they have been meaning to do if they only had time.

Thirdly are the 'fidgets', these are usually the majority of us and spend their journey trying to be a 'snorer' and wondering why they cant get to sleep. A 'fidget' will keep themselves amused for short periods by doing different activities, but get bored easily.

This is where I end the book so I'll leave you thinking about which type of passenger you are. Hopefully you have learned something and found answers to most of your questions and been directed to web sites and other resources which will help you plan, prepare and endure what can be a tiresome but exciting adventure.

Have a great time!

# Tiny URL's

Throughout this publication a Tiny URL has been used to shorten long web site addresses where considered appropriate.

Http://www.tinyurl.com is a free to use service.

The original web site addresses made short are as follows:

**Page 19**

*http://tinyurl.com/6gptwo*

http://www.undercovertourist.com/united-states/florida/orlando/attractions/when-to-visit.html

**Page 32**

*http://tinyurl.com/5eebe4*

http://www.citizensadvice.org.uk/index/pressoffice/press_index/press_060816.htm

**Page 46**

*http://tinyurl.com/62shhz*

http://matadorstudy.com/10-japanese-customs-you-must-know-before-a-trip-to-japan/

**Page 81**

*http://tinyurl.com/3drcdf*

http://www.youtube.com/watch?v=UdeMLfvHcrU

*http://tinyurl.com/2ua3jj*

http://www.youtube.com/watch?v=s-hJtGj4u1k

**Page 85**

*http://tinyurl.com/ptxdw*

http://www.tsa.gov/travelers/airtravel/prohibited/permitted-prohibited-items.shtm

*http://tinyurl.com/2ock3m*

http://www.youtube.com/watch?v=McB9f6dETL0

*http://tinyurl.com/2l9gy2*

http://www.youtube.com/watch?v=Pp1yTDmlgVw&

**Page 97**

*http://tinyurl.com/3lw6ut*

http://travel.howstuffworks.com/airport-security3.htm

**Page 99**

*http://tinyurl.com/5d9rrd*

http://www.mattheweaves.co.uk/2005/04/19/airport

**Page 100**

*http://tinyurl.com/62zz46*

http://news.bbc.co.uk/1/hi/business/4271197.stm

**Page 101**

*http://tinyurl.com/4vorx3*

http://www.airsafe.com/complain/bumping.htm

**Page 119**

*http://tinyurl.com/6kwrwy*

http://www.youtube.com/watch?v=alh_2xg5GWo

**Page 121**

*http://tinyurl.com/57pab4*

http://www.ehow.com/how_3712_exercise-plane.html

**Page 123**

*http://tinyurl.com/3w8x4a*

http://www.ind.homeoffice.gov.uk/visitingtheuk

# Further Reading

Bearman, E. 2008, Traveling Solo: Advice and Ideas for More Than 250 Great Vacations, ISBN: 978-0762747931.

Foster, S. 2008, Smart Packing for Today's Traveler, ISBN: 978-0970219671.

Gilford, J. 2006, Packing Book: Secrets of the Carry-on Traveler, ISBN: 978-1580087834.

Harding, M. 2003, Weather to Travel: The Traveller's Guide to the World's Weather, ISBN: 978-1858900292.

King, K. & Robertson, E. 2008, The Backpacker's Bible Revised Edition, ISBN: 978-1906032272.

Lansky, D. 2008, The Rough Guide to the First-Time Around the World - Edition 2, ISBN: 978-1843536611.

Rasheed de Francisco, F. 2008, The Rough Guide to Travel with Babies and Young Children, ISBN: 978-1843537045.

Roach Jr, J. P. 2007, Around the World In A Wheel Chair: A Motivational Adventure For the Disabled, ISBN: 978-1434341426.

Roberts, R. B., Philbin, A. & Groenewege, A. D. 2001, Air Travel Guide for Seniors and Disabled Passengers: Useful Tips, Planning AIDS and Resources for Air Travelers with Reduced Mobility or Special Medical Condiations, ISBN: 978-0968078327.

Sangster, R. 2000, Traveler's Tool Kit, ISBN: 978-0897323413.

World Health Organisation. 2008, International Travel and Health 2008: Situation as on 1 January 2008, ISBN: 978-9241580403.

# Notes

If you have some advice or a tip that has not been included in this book, which could be considered for the third edition; please post it along with your name and location on the http://www. longhaulflighttips.net website.

# Index

Printed in the United States
218594BV00001B/220/P